The Seven Last Words Spoken By Christ On The Cross, Tr. From The Lat

You are holding a reproduction of an original work that is in the public domain in the United States of America, and possibly other countries. You may freely copy and distribute this work as no entity (individual or corporate) has a copyright on the body of the work. This book may contain prior copyright references, and library stamps (as most of these works were scanned from library copies). These have been scanned and retained as part of the historical artifact.

This book may have occasional imperfections such as missing or blurred pages, poor pictures, errant marks, etc. that were either part of the original artifact, or were introduced by the scanning process. We believe this work is culturally important, and despite the imperfections, have elected to bring it back into print as part of our continuing commitment to the preservation of printed works worldwide. We appreciate your understanding of the imperfections in the preservation process, and hope you enjoy this valuable book.

THE SEVEN WORDS.

The Seven Words

SPOKEN BY CHRIST ON THE CROSS.

BY

CARDINAL BELLARMINE.

Translated from the Latin.

REPRINTED FROM THE "MESSENGER OF THE SACRED HEART."

LONDON:
BURNS AND OATES, PORTMAN STREET,
AND PATERNOSTER ROW.

1877.

ROEHAMPTON:
PRINTED BY JAMES STANLEY.

PREFACE.

BEHOLD me, now, for the fourth year, preparing for my death. Having withdrawn from the business of the world to a place of repose, I give myself up to the meditation of the Sacred Scriptures, and to writing the thoughts that occur to me in my meditations; so that if I am no longer able to be of use by word of mouth, or the composition of voluminous works, I may at least be of some use to my brethren, by these pious little books. Whilst then I was reflecting as to what would be the most eligible subject both to prepare me to die well, and to assist others to live well, the death of our Lord occurred to me, together with the last sermon which the Redeemer of the world preached from the Cross, as from an elevated pulpit, to the human race. This sermon consists of seven short but weighty sentences, and in these seven words is comprised everything of which our Lord spoke when He said: "*Behold we go up to Jerusalem, and all things shall be accomplished which were written by the Prophets concerning the Son of Man.*"* The things which the Prophets foretold about Christ may be reduced to four heads: His sermons to the people; His prayer to His Father; the great torments He endured; and the sublime and admirable works He performed. Now these things were verified in a wonderful manner in the Life of Christ, for our Lord was ever most diligent in preaching to the people. He preached in the Temple, in

* St. Luke xviii. 31.

the synagogues, in the fields, in deserts, in private houses, nay, He preached even from a ship to the people who were standing on the shore. It was His wont to spend nights in prayer to GOD: for so says the Evangelist: "*He passed the whole night in the prayer of God.*"* His admirable works of casting out devils, of curing the sick, of multiplying loaves, of allaying storms,† are to be read in every page of the Gospels. Again, the injuries that were heaped upon Him, in return for the good He had done, were many. They consisted not only in contumelious words, but also in stoning‡ and in casting Him down headlong.§ In a word, all these things were truly consummated on the Cross. His preaching from the Cross was so powerful that "*all the multitude returned striking their breasts,*"∥ and not only the hearts of men but even rocks were rent asunder. He prayed on the Cross, as the Apostle says, "*with a strong cry and tears,*" so that He "*was heard for His reverence.*"¶ He suffered so much on the Cross in comparison to what He had suffered during the rest of His life that suffering seems only to belong to His Passion. Finally, He never wrought greater signs and prodigies than when on the Cross He seemed to be reduced to the greatest weakness and infirmity. He then not only showed signs from heaven, which the Jews had previously asked of Him even to importunity, but a little while after He showed the greatest of all signs. For after He was dead and buried He rose again from the dead by His own power, recalling His Body to life, even to an immortal life. Truly then may we say that on the Cross was consummated everything that had been written by the Prophets concerning the Son of Man.

But before I begin to write on the words which our Lord spoke from the Cross, it seems proper that I should

---

* St. Luke vi. 12.   † St. Matt. viii.; St. Mark iv.; St. Luke vi.; St. John vi.
‡ St. John viii.   § St. Luke iv.   ∥ St. Luke xxiii. 48.   ¶ Heb. v. 7.

say something of the Cross itself, which was the pulpit of the Preacher, the altar of the Sacrificing Priest, the arena of the Combatant, the workshop of the Wonder-worker. The ancients commonly agree in saying that the cross was made of three pieces of wood; one upright, along which the body of the crucified person was stretched; another transverse, to which the hands were fastened; and the third was attached to the lower part of the cross, on which the feet of the condemned rested, but fastened by nails to prevent their moving about. The ancient Fathers of the Church agree in this opinion, as St. Justin * and St. Irenæus.† These authors, moreover, clearly indicate that each foot rested on the foot-board, and that one foot was not placed over the other. Hence it follows that Christ was nailed to the Cross with four nails, and not with three, as many imagine, who in pictures represent Christ, our Lord, as nailed to the Cross with one foot over the other. Gregory of Tours,‡ distinctly says the contrary, and confirms his view by an appeal to ancient pictures. I, for my part, have seen in the Royal Library at Paris, some very ancient manuscripts of the Gospels, which contained many pictures of Christ crucified, and these all had the four nails.

St. Augustin,§ and St. Gregory of Nyssa,|| say that the upright piece of the Cross projected a little from the transverse piece. It would seem that the Apostle also insinuates the same, for in his Epistle to the Ephesians St. Paul writes: "*That you may be able to comprehend with all the saints, what is the breadth, and length, and height, and depth.*"¶ This is clearly a description of the figure of the Cross, which has four extremes; breadth in the transverse piece; length in the upright piece; height in that part of the

---

* In *Dial. cum Thyphon*, lib. v.   † *Advers. hæres. Valent.*
‡ *Lib. de Gloria Martyr.* c. vi.   § Epist. i. || Serm. i. *De Ressur.*
¶ Ephes. iii. 18.

Cross which stood out and projected from the transverse part; and depth in the part which was buried in the earth. Our Lord did not endure the torments of the Cross by chance, or unwillingly, since He had chosen this kind of death from all eternity, as St. Augustine* teaches from the testimony of the Apostle: "*Jesus of Nazareth being delivered up, by the determinate counsel and foreknowledge of God, you by the hands of wicked men have crucified and slain.*"† And so Christ, at the beginning of His preaching, said to Nicodemus: "*As Moses lifted up the serpent in the desert, so must the Son of Man be lifted up: that whosoever believeth in Him may not perish, but may have life everlasting.*"‡ He often spoke to His Apostles about His Cross, and encouraged them to imitate Him by the words: "*If any man will come after Me, let him deny himself, and take up his cross and follow Me.*"§

Our Lord alone knows the reason that induced Him to choose this manner of death. The holy Fathers, however, have thought of some mystical reasons, and have left them to us in their writings. St. Irenæus, in the work of his to which we have referred, says that the words, "JESUS OF NAZARETH, KING OF THE JEWS," were written over that part of the Cross where the two arms meet, to give us to understand, that the two nations, of Jew and Gentile, which had up to that time been estranged from each other, were henceforth to be united into one body under the one Head, Christ. St. Gregory of Nyssa, in his sermon on the Resurrection, says that the part of the Cross which looked towards heaven, shows that heaven is to be opened by the Cross as by a key; that the part which was buried in the earth shows that hell was despoiled by Christ when He descended thither; and that the two arms of the Cross, which stretched towards the east and west, show the regeneration of the whole world by the Blood of Christ.

* Epist. 120. † Acts ii. 23. ‡ St. John iii. 14, 15. § St. Matt. xvi. 24.

St. Jerome, on the Epistle to the Ephesians, St. Augustine,* in his Epistle to Honoratus, St. Bernard, in the fifth book of his work on *Consideration*, teach that the principal mystery of the Cross was briefly touched upon by the Apostle in the words: "*What is the breadth, and length, and height, and depth.*"† The primary signification of these words points to the attributes of GOD; the height signifies His power; the depth, His wisdom; the breadth, His goodness; the length, His eternity. They have reference also to the virtues of Christ in His Passion; the breadth, His charity; the length, His patience; the height, His obedience; the depth, His humility. They signify, moreover, the virtues which are necessary for those who are saved through Christ. The depth of the Cross means faith; the height, hope; the breadth, charity; the length, perseverance. From this we gather that only charity, the queen of virtues, finds a place everywhere, in GOD, in Christ, and in ourselves. Of the other virtues, some are proper to GOD, others to Christ, and others to us. Consequently it is not wonderful that in His last words from the Cross, which we are now going to explain, Christ should give the first place to words of charity.

We shall therefore begin by explaining the first three words which were spoken by Christ about the sixth hour, before the sun was obscured and darkness overspread the earth. We shall then consider this eclipse of the sun, and finally come to the explanation of the other words of our Lord, which were spoken about the ninth hour,‡ when the darkness was disappearing, and the death of Christ was at hand.

* Epist. 120.   † Ephes. iii. 18.   ‡ St. Matt. xxvii.

CONTENTS.

BOOK I.

On the First Three Words spoken on the Cross.

	Page
Chapter I.—The literal explanation of the first word, "Father, forgive them, for they know not what they do"	1
Chapter II.—The first fruit to be drawn from the consideration of the first word spoken by Christ upon the Cross	8
Chapter III.—The second fruit to be drawn from the consideration of the first word spoken by Christ upon the Cross	12
Chapter IV.—The literal explanation of the second word, "Amen, I say to Thee, this day thou shalt be with Me in Paradise"	19
Chapter V. The first fruit to be drawn from the consideration of the second word spoken by Christ upon the Cross	29
Chapter VI.—The second fruit to be drawn from the consideration of the second word spoken by Christ upon the Cross	32
Chapter VII.—The third fruit to be drawn from the consideration of the second word spoken by Christ upon the Cross	35
Chapter VIII.—The literal explanation of the third word, "Behold thy Mother: behold thy Son"	42
Chapter IX.—The first fruit to be drawn from the consideration of the third word spoken by Christ upon the Cross	47
Chapter X.—The second fruit to be drawn from the consideration of the third word spoken by Christ upon the Cross	49
Chapter XI.—The third fruit to be drawn from the consideration of the third word spoken by Christ upon the Cross	52
Chapter XII.—The fourth fruit to be drawn from the consideration of the third word spoken by Christ upon the Cross	59

BOOK II.

On the Last Four Words spoken on the Cross.

	Page
Chapter I.—The literal explanation of the fourth word, "My God, my God, why hast thou abandoned Me."	67
Chapter II.—The first fruit to be drawn from the consideration of the fourth word spoken by Christ upon the Cross.	74
Chapter III.—The second fruit to be drawn from the consideration of the fourth word spoken by Christ upon the Cross	76
Chapter IV.—The third fruit to be drawn from the consideration of the fourth word spoken by Christ upon the Cross.	78
Chapter V.—The fourth fruit to be drawn from the consideration of the fourth word spoken by Christ upon the Cross.	82
Chapter VI.—The fifth fruit to be drawn from the consideration of the fourth word spoken by Christ upon the Cross.	86
Chapter VII.—The literal explanation of the fifth word, "I thirst"	90
Chapter VIII.—The first fruit to be drawn from the consideration of the fifth word spoken by Christ upon the Cross.	93
Chapter IX.—The second fruit to be drawn from the consideration of the fifth word spoken by Christ upon the Cross.	99
Chapter X.—The third fruit to be drawn from the consideration of the fifth word spoken by Christ upon the Cross	100
Chapter XI.—The fourth fruit to be drawn from the consideration of the fifth word spoken by Christ upon the Cross.	111
Chapter XII.—The literal explanation of the sixth word, "It is consummated"	114
Chapter XIII.—The first fruit to be drawn from the consideration of the sixth word spoken by Christ upon the Cross.	124
Chapter XIV.—The second fruit to be drawn from the consideration of the sixth word spoken by Christ upon the Cross	126
Chapter XV.—The third fruit to be drawn from the consideration of the sixth word spoken by Christ upon the Cross	128
Chapter XVI.—The fourth fruit to be drawn from the consideration of the sixth word spoken by Christ upon the Cross	134

	Page
Chapter XVII.—The fifth fruit to be drawn from the consideration of the sixth word spoken by Christ upon the Cross	136
Chapter XVIII.—The sixth fruit to be drawn from the consideration of the sixth word spoken by Christ upon the Cross	137
Chapter XIX.—The literal explanation of the seventh word, "Father, into Thy hands I commend My Spirit"	144
Chapter XX. The first fruit to be drawn from the consideration of the seventh word spoken by Christ upon the Cross	148
Chapter XXI.—The second fruit to be drawn from the consideration of the seventh word spoken by Christ upon the Cross	151
Chapter XXII.—The third fruit to be drawn from the consideration of the seventh word spoken by Christ upon the Cross	155
Chapter XXIII.—The fourth fruit to be drawn from the consideration of the seventh word spoken by Christ upon the Cross	157
Chapter XXIV.—The last fruit to be drawn from the consideration of the seventh word spoken by Christ upon the Cross	160

BOOK I.

On the First Three Words spoken on the Cross.

On the First Three Words spoken on the Cross.

CHAPTER I.

The literal explanation of the first word, "Father, forgive them, for they know not what they do."

CHRIST JESUS, the Word of the Eternal Father, of Whom the Father Himself hath spoken, "*Hear ye Him,*"* and Who hath said of Himself, "*For one is your master, Christ,*"† in order to perform the task He had undertaken, never ceased from instructing us. Not only during His life, but even in the arms of death, from the pulpit of the Cross, He preached to us words few in number, but burning with love, most useful and efficacious, and in every way worthy to be engraven on the heart of every Christian, to be preserved there, meditated upon, and fulfilled literally and in deed. His first word is this, "*And Jesus said: Father, forgive them, for they know not what they do.*"‡ Which prayer, as though it were altogether new and unheard of before, the Holy Spirit wished to be foretold by the Prophet Isaias in these words: "*And He prayed for the evil doers.*" § And the petitions of our Lord on the Cross prove how truly the Apostle St. Paul spoke when he said: "*Charity seeketh not her own,*" ‖ for of the seven words our Redeemer spoke three were for the good of others, three for His own good, and one was common both to Himself and to

---
* St. Matt. xvii. 5.   † St. Matt. xxiii. 10.   ‡ St. Luke xxiii. 34.
§ Isaias liii. 12.   ‖ 1 Cor. xiii. 5.

us. His first care, however, was for others. He thought of Himself last.

Of the first three words which He spoke, the first was for His enemies, the second for His friends, the third for His relations. Now, the reason why He thus prayed, is that the first demand of charity is to succour those who are in want: and those who were then most in want of spiritual succour were His enemies; and what we also, the disciples of so great a Master, stand most in need of is to love our enemies, a virtue which we know is most difficult to be obtained and rarely to be met with, whereas the love of our friends and relations is easy and natural, increases with our years, and often predominates more than it ought. Wherefore the Evangelist wrote, "*And Jesus said:*"* where the word *and* shows the time and the occasion of this prayer for His enemies, and places in contrast the words of the Sufferer and the words of the executioners, His works and their works; as though the Evangelist would explain himself more fully thus: they were crucifying the Lord, and in His very presence were dividing His garments amongst them, they mocked and defamed Him as a seducer and a liar; whilst He, seeing what they were doing, hearing what they were saying, and suffering the most acute pains in His hands and feet, returned good for evil and prayed; "*Father, forgive them.*"

He calls Him *Father*, not GOD or Lord, because He wished Him to exercise the benignity of a Father and not the severity of a Judge; and as He desired to avert the anger of GOD, which He knew was aroused at their enormous crimes, He uses the tender name of Father. The word Father appears to contain in itself this bequest: I, your Son, in the midst of all My torments have pardoned them; do you likewise, My Father, extend

* St. Luke xxiii. 34.

your pardon to them. Although they deserve it not, still pardon them for the sake of Me, your Son. Remember, too, that you are their Father, since you have created them, and made them to your own image and likeness. Show them therefore a Father's love, for although they are wicked, they are nevertheless your children.

Forgive. This word contains the chief petition which the Son of GOD, as the advocate for His enemies, made to His Father. The word *Forgive* may be referred both to the punishment due to the crime as well as to the crime itself. If it be referred to the punishment due to the crime, then was the prayer heard: for since this sin of the Jews demanded that its perpetrators should be instantly and condignly made to feel the wrath of GOD, by either being consumed with fire from heaven, or drowned in a second deluge, or extirpated with famine and the sword, still the infliction of this punishment was postponed for forty years, during which period, if the Jewish people had done penance they would have been saved and their city preserved, but because they did not perform penance, GOD sent against them the Roman army, which, in the reign of Vespasian, destroyed their metropolis, and partly by famine during the siege, and partly by the sword in the sack of the city, slew a vast multitude of its inhabitants, whilst the survivors were sold into slavery and scattered throughout the world. All these misfortunes were foretold by our Lord in the parables of the householder who hired labourers for his vineyard; of the king who made a marriage for his son; of the barren fig-tree; and more clearly when He wept over the city on Palm Sunday. Our Lord's prayer was also heard if it have reference to the crime of the Jews, since it obtained for many the grace of compunction and of reformation of life. There were some who "*returned striking their breasts.*"[*] There

---

[*] St. Luke xxiii. 48.

was the Centurion, who said, "*Truly this was the Son of God.*"* And there were many who a few weeks afterwards were converted by the preaching of the Apostles, and confessed Him Whom they denied, adored Him Whom they had despised. But the reason why the grace of conversion was not granted to all is that the will of Christ was conformable to the wisdom and the will of GOD, which St. Luke shows us when he says in the Acts of the Apostles, "*As many as were ordained to life everlasting, believed.*"†

Them. This word applied to all for whose pardon Christ prayed. In the first place it is applied to those who really nailed Christ to the Cross, and cast lots for His garments. It may also be extended to all who were the cause of our Lord's Passion: to Pilate who pronounced the sentence; to the people who cried out, "*Away with Him, away with Him, crucify Him;*"‡ to the chief priests and the scribes who falsely accused him; and, to proceed still farther, to the first man and all his posterity who by their sins occasioned Christ's death. And thus from His Cross our Lord prayed for the forgiveness of all His enemies. Each one, however, may reckon himself amongst the enemies of Christ according to the words of the Apostle, "*When we were enemies we were reconciled to God by the death of His Son.*"§ Therefore our High Priest Christ made a commemoration for all of us, even before our birth, in that most holy *Memento*, if I may so speak, which He made in the first Sacrifice of the Mass which He celebrated on the altar of the Cross. What return then, O my soul, wilt thou make to the Lord for all that He hath done for thee, even before thou hadst a being? Our dear Lord saw that thou also wouldst one day rank thyself with His enemies, and though thou askedst not,

---

* St. Matt. xxvii. 54.   † Acts. xiii. 48.   ‡ St. Matt. xxvii. 22.
§ Rom. v. 10.

not besoughtest Him, He prayed for thee to His Father not to lay to thy charge the fault of folly. Does it not therefore behove thee to bear in mind so sweet a Patron, and to make every effort to serve Him faithfully in all things? Is it not just that with such an example before thee thou shouldst learn not only to pardon thy enemies with ease, and to pray for them, but even bring as many as thou canst to do the same? It is just, and this I desire and purpose to do, provided that He Who has set me so brilliant an example would also in His goodness give me sufficient help to accomplish so great a work.

For they know not what they do. In order that His prayer might be reasonable, Christ extenuates, or rather gives what excuse He could for the sins of His enemies. He certainly could not excuse either the injustice of Pilate, or the cruelty of the soldiers, or the ingratitude of the people, or the false testimony of those who perjured themselves. It only remained for Him then to excuse their fault on the plea of ignorance. For with truth does the Apostle observe, "*If they had known it, they would never have crucified the Lord of glory.*"* Neither Pilate, nor the chief priests, nor the people knew that Christ was the Lord of glory, still Pilate knew Him to be a just and holy man, Who had been delivered up through the envy of the chief priests; and the chief priests knew Him to be the promised Christ, as St. Thomas teaches, because they neither could nor did they deny that He had wrought many of the miracles which the prophets foretold the Messias would work. In fine, the people knew that Christ had been unjustly condemned, since Pilate publicly told them, "*I find no cause in this Man:*" † and, "*I am innocent of the blood of this just Man.*"‡ But although the Jews, both priests and people, ignored the fact that Christ was the Lord of glory, nevertheless, they

---

* 1 Cor. ii. 8. † St. Luke xxiii. 14. ‡ St. Matt. xxvii. 24.

would not have remained in this state of ignorance if their malice had not blinded them. According to the words of St. John: "*And whereas He had done so many miracles before them, they believed not in Him, because Isaias said: He hath blinded their eyes, and hardened their heart, that they should not see with their eyes, nor understand with their heart, and be converted, and I should heal them.*"* Blindness is no excuse for a blind man, because it is voluntary, always accompanies him and does not precede him. Similarly those who sin in the malice of their hearts may always plead their ignorance, which is nevertheless not an excuse for their sin since it does not precede it but accompanies it. Wherefore the Wise Man says, "*They err who work iniquity.*"† The Philosopher likewise with truth proclaims every evil-doer to be ignorant of what he does, and consequently it may ingeniously be said of sinners in general, "*They know not what they do.*" For no one can desire that which is wicked on the ground of its wickedness, because the will of man does not tend to what is bad as well as to what is good, but solely to what is good, and for this reason those who make choice of what is bad do so because the object is presented to them under the aspect of something good, and may thus be selected. This results from the disquietude of the inferior part of the soul which blinds the reason and renders it incapable of distinguishing anything but what is good in the object it seeks. Thus the man who commits adultery or is guilty of a theft perpetrates these crimes because he looks only to the pleasure or the gain which may result, and he would not perpetrate them if his passions had not blinded him to the shameful infamy of the one and the injustice of the other. Hence a sinner is like to a man who wishes to throw himself from an eminence into a river, he just shuts his eyes and then casts himself

* St. John xii. 37—40.   † Prov. xiv. 22.

headlong; so he who does an evil act hates the light, and labours under a voluntary ignorance which does not exculpate him, because it is voluntary. But if voluntary ignorance does not exculpate the sinner, why did our Lord pray, "*Forgive them, for they know not what they do*"? To this I answer that the most straightforward interpretation to be put to our Lord's words is that they were spoken for His executioners, who were probably entirely ignorant not only of our Lord's Divinity, but even of His innocence, and simply performed the hangman's duty. For those, therefore, our Lord most truly said, "*Father, forgive them, for they know not what they do.*"

Again, if our Lord's prayer be interpreted as applicable to ourselves who had not then a being, or to that multitude of sinners who were His contemporaries, but had no knowledge of what was being enacted in Jerusalem, then did our Lord most truly say, "*They know not what they do.*" Lastly, if He addressed His Father in behalf of those who were present, and knew that Christ was the Messias and an innocent Man, then must we confess the charity of Christ to be such as to wish to palliate as far as possible the sin of His enemies. If ignorance cannot justify a fault, it may nevertheless serve as a trivial excuse, and the deicide of the Jews would have worn a more heinous aspect had they known the character of their Victim. Although our Lord was aware that this was not so much an excuse as a shadow of an excuse, He urged it forsooth to show us how kindly He feels towards the sinner, and how eagerly He would have used a better defence even for Caiphas and Pilate, had a better and more reasonable apology presented itself.

CHAPTER II.

The first fruit to be drawn from the consideration of the first word spoken by Christ upon the Cross.

Having given the literal meaning of the first word spoken by our Lord on the Cross, our next endeavour must be to gather some of its most eligible and advantageous fruits. What strikes us most in the first part of Christ's sermon on the Cross is His ardent charity which burns with a more brilliant lustre than we can either know or conceive, according to that which St. Paul wrote to the Ephesians, saying, "*To know also the charity of Christ which surpasseth all knowledge.*"* For in this passage the Apostle informs us by the mystery of the Cross how the charity of Christ surpasseth our understanding because it extends beyond the compass of our limited intellect. For when we suffer any grievous pain, as for example a toothache, or a headache, or a pain in the eyes, or in any other member of our body, our mind is so rivetted on this as to be incapable of any exertion; hence we are in no humour either to receive our friends, or carry on our business. But when Christ was nailed to the Cross He wore His diadem of thorns, as is clearly shown in the writings of the ancient Fathers; by Tertullian amongst the Latin Fathers in his book against the Jews, and amongst the Greek Fathers by Origen in his work upon St. Matthew, and hence it followed that He could neither lean His head back, nor move it from side to side without additional pain. Rough nails held fast His hands and feet, and from the manner in which they tore their way through His flesh occasioned a most acute and lasting torment. His body was naked, worn out with the cruel scourging and

* Ephes. iii. 19.

the journeyings to and fro, ignominiously exposed to the gaze of the vulgar, and by its weight was widening with a barbarous and continual agony the wounds in His hands and feet; all which things combined were the source of much suffering, and as it were of additional crosses. Yet, O charity! truly surpassing our understanding, He thought no more of His torments than if He were suffering nothing, and is solicitous only for the salvation of His enemies; and desiring to screen them from the penalty of their crimes, cries aloud to His Father, "*Father, forgive them.*" What would He have done if these wretches had been the victims of an unjust persecution, or had been His friends, His relations, or His children, and not His enemies, His betrayers and abandoned parricides? Truly, O most benign JESUS! your charity surpasses our understanding. I behold your Heart in the midst of such a storm of injuries and sufferings, like a rock in the midst of the ocean which remains immoveable and at rest, though the billows dash themselves in fury against it. For you see your enemies are not satisfied with inflicting mortal wounds on your body, but must scoff at your patience, and howl in triumph at your ill-treatment; you look upon them, I say, not as a foe scans his antagonists, but as a father regards his wandering children, as a doctor listens to the ravings of a delirious patient. Wherefore you are not angry with them but pity them, and intrust them to the care of your all-powerful Father, that He would cure them and make them whole. This is the effect of true charity, to be on good terms with all men, to consider no one your enemy, and to live at peace with those who hate peace.

This is what is sung in the canticle of love about the virtue of perfect charity. "*Many waters cannot quench charity, neither can the floods drown it.*"* The many waters are the many sufferings which our spiritual miseries,

---

* Cant. viii. 7.

like storms of hell, let loose on Christ through the instrumentality of the Jews and Gentiles, who represented the dark passions of our heart. Still this deluge of waters, that is of dolours, could not extinguish the fire of charity which burnt in the breast of Christ. Therefore the charity of Christ was greater than this deluge of many waters, and it shone brilliantly in His prayer, "*Father, forgive them.*" And not only were these many waters incapable of extinguishing the charity of Christ, but neither in after ages were the storms of persecution able to overwhelm the charity of the members of Christ. Thus the charity of Christ, which possessed the heart of St. Stephen, could not be crushed out by the stones wherewith he was martyred; it was alive there, and he prayed, "*Lord, lay not this sin to their charge.*"* In fine, the perfect and invincible charity of Christ which has been propagated in the hearts of many thousands of martyrs and confessors, has so stoutly combated the attacks of visible and invisible persecutors, that it may be said with truth even to the end of the world, that a sea of suffering shall not extinguish the flame of charity.

But from the consideration of the Humanity of Christ let us ascend to the consideration of His Divinity. Great was the charity of Christ as Man towards His executioners, but greater still will be the charity of Christ as GOD, and of the Father, and of the Holy Ghost, at the last day towards all mankind who have been guilty of acts of enmity towards their Creator, and would, had they been able, have cast Him out of heaven, have nailed Him to a cross, and have slain Him. Who can conceive the charity which GOD bears towards such ungrateful and wicked creatures? GOD did not spare the angels when they sinned, nor did He give them time for repentance, but He often bears patiently with sinful men, with blas-

* Acts vii. 59.

phemers, and with those who enrol themselves under the standard of the devil, His enemy; and He not only bears with them, but meanwhile feeds them and nourishes them, even supports and sustains them, for "*in Him we live and move and are,*"* as the Apostle says. Nor does He preserve the good and the just only, but likewise the ungrateful and the wicked, as our Lord informs us in the Gospel of St. Luke. Nor does our good Lord merely feed and nourish, support and sustain His enemies, but He often heaps His favours upon them, gives them talent, increases their riches, makes them honourable, and raises them to temporal thrones, whilst He all the while patiently awaits their return from the path of iniquity and perdition.

And to pass over several characteristics of the charity which GOD feels towards wicked men, the enemies of His Divine Majesty, each one of which would require a volume if we dwelt upon them singly, we will confine ourselves at present to that singular kindness of Christ of which we were treating. "*For has not God so loved the world as to give His only-begotten Son?*"† The world is the enemy of GOD, for "*the whole world is seated in wickedness,*"‡ as St. John tells us; and "*if any man love the world the charity of the Father is not in him,*"§ as he says again in another place. St. James writes, "*Whosoever therefore will be a friend of this world, becometh an enemy of God,*" and "*the friendship of this world is the enmity of God.*"∥ GOD therefore in loving this world cherishes His enemy with the intention of making it His friend. For this purpose has He sent His Son, "*the Prince of Peace,*"¶ that by His means the world might be reconciled to GOD. Therefore at the birth of Christ the angels sang, "*Glory to God in the highest, and on earth peace.*"** Thus

---

* Acts xvii. 28.
† St. John iii. 16.   ‡ 1 St. John v. 19.   § 1 St. John ii. 15.
∥ St. James iv. 4.   ¶ Isaias ii. 6.   ** St. Luke ii. 14.

GOD has loved the world, His enemy, and has taken the first step towards peace, by giving to it His Son, Who might bring about the reconciliation by suffering the penalty due to His enemy. The world received not Christ, increased its guilt, rebelled against the one Mediator, and GOD inspired this Mediator to return good for evil by praying for His persecutors. He prayed and "*was heard for His reverence.*"* GOD patiently awaited to see what progress the Apostles would make by their preaching in the conversion of the world; those who did penance received pardon; those who repented not after such patient forbearance were exterminated by GOD's just judgment. Therefore from this first word of Christ we really learn that the charity of GOD the Father, Who "*so loved the world as to give His only-begotten Son, that whosoever believeth in Him may not perish but may have life everlasting,*"† surpasses all knowledge.

CHAPTER III.

The second fruit to be drawn from the consideration of the first word spoken by Christ upon the Cross.

If men would learn to pardon without a murmur the injuries they receive, and thus force their enemies to become their friends, we might learn a second and very salutary lesson by meditating on the first word. The example of Christ and the Blessed Trinity ought to be a powerful argument to persuade us to this. For if Christ forgave and prayed for His executioners, what reason can be alleged why a Christian should not act similarly to his enemies? If GOD, our Creator, the Lord and Judge of all men, Who has it in His power to take instant vengeance

* Heb. v. 7.   † St. John iii. 16.

on a sinner, awaits his return to repentance, and invites him to peace and reconciliation with the promise of pardoning his treasons against the Divine Majesty, why should not a creature imitate this conduct, particularly if we remember that the pardon of an insult merits a great reward? We read in the history of St. Engelbert, Archbishop of Cologne, who was murdered by some enemies who were lying in wait for him, that at the moment of his death he prayed for them in the words of our Lord, "*Father, forgive them;*" and it was revealed that this action was so pleasing to GOD, that his soul was carried by the hands of angels to heaven, and placed amongst the choir of martyrs, where he received the martyr's crown and palm ; and his tomb was rendered famous by the working of many miracles.

Oh, if Christians would learn how easily they can, if they wish, acquire inexhaustible treasures, and merit signal degrees of honour and glory by gaining the mastery over the various agitations of their souls, and magnanimously despising small and trivial insults, they would certainly not be so hard-hearted and obstinately set against pardon and forgiveness. They argue that they would act against nature to allow themselves to be unjustly spurned and outraged by word and deed. For wild animals, which merely follow the instinct of nature, fiercely attack their enemies the moment they behold them, and kill them either with their teeth or their claws ; so we, at the sight of our enemy, feel our blood beginning to boil, and our desire of revenge is aroused. Such reasoning is false ; it does not draw a distinction between self-defence which is lawful, and a spirit of revenge which is unlawful.

No one can find fault with a man who defends himself in just cause, and nature teaches us to repel force by force, but it does not teach us to take upon ourselves to avenge an injury we have received. No one hinders us from taking precautions necessary to provide against an attack, but the law of GOD forbids us to be revengeful. To punish an injustice belongs not to the private individual but to the public magistrate, and because GOD is the King of kings, therefore does He cry out and say, "*Revenge to Me; I will repay.*"*

As to the argument that one animal is carried by its very nature to attack the animal which is the enemy of its species, I answer that this is the result of their being irrational animals, which cannot distinguish between nature and what is vicious in nature. But men who are endowed with reason ought to draw a line between the nature or the person which has been created by GOD and is good, and the vice or the sin which is bad and does not proceed from GOD. Accordingly, when a man has been insulted, he ought to love the person of his enemy and hate the insult, and should rather have pity on him than be angry with him; just as a physician who loves his patients and prescribes for them with due care, but hates the disease, and endeavours with all the resources at his command to drive it away, to destroy it and render it harmless. And this is what the Master and Physician of our souls, Christ our Lord, teaches when He says, "*Love your enemies; do good to them that hate you, and pray for them that persecute and calumniate you.*"† Christ our Master is not like the Scribes and Pharisees who sat in the chair of Moses and taught, but did not put their teaching in practice. When He ascended the pulpit of the Cross He practised what He taught, by praying aloud for the enemies whom He loved, "*Father, forgive them, for they know not what they do.*" Now, the reason why the sight of an enemy makes the blood boil in the very veins of some people is this, that they are animals who have not yet learnt to bring the motions of the inferior part of the soul, which are common

---

* Rom. xii. 19.   † St. Matt. v. 44.

both to mankind and to the brute creation, under the domain of reason; whereas spiritual men are not subject to these motions of the flesh, but know how to keep them in check; are not angry with those who have injured them, but, on the contrary, pity them, and by showing them acts of kindness strive to bring them to peace and unity.

But this it is objected is too difficult and severe a trial for men of noble birth, who ought to be solicitous for their honour. Nay rather, the task is an easy one; for, as the Evangelist testifies, "*the yoke*" of Christ, Who has laid down this law for the guidance of His followers, "*is sweet, and His burden light;*" * and "*His commandments are not heavy,*" as St. John affirms.† And if they appear difficult and severe, they appear so because we have little or no love for GOD, for nothing is difficult to him who loves, according to the saying of the Apostle: "*Charity is patient, is kind, beareth all things, believeth all things, hopeth all things, endureth all things.*"‡ Nor is Christ the only one Who has loved His enemies, although in the perfection with which He practised the virtue He has surpassed every one else, for the holy Patriarch Joseph loved with a singular love his brethren who sold him into slavery. And in the Holy Scripture we read how David most patiently put up with the persecutions of his enemy Saul, who for a long time sought his death, and when it was in the power of David to take away the life of Saul he did not slay him. And under the law of grace the protomartyr, St. Stephen, imitated the example of Christ by making this prayer when he was being stoned to death: "*Lord, lay not this sin to their charge;*" § and St. James the Apostle, the Bishop of Jerusalem, who was cast headlong from the battlements of the Temple, cried to heaven in the moment of his death, "*Lord, pardon them, for they*

---

* St. Matt. xi. 39.   † 1 St. John v. 3.   ‡ 1 Cor. xiii. 4—7.
§ Acts vii. 59.

know not what they do." And St. Paul writes of himself and of his fellow-Apostles: *" We are reviled and we bless; we are persecuted and we suffer it; we are blasphemed and we entreat."* * In fine, many martyrs and innumerable others, after the example of Christ, have found no difficulty in fulfilling this commandment. But there may be some who will further argue: I do not deny that we must pardon our enemies, but I will choose my own time for doing so, when forsooth I have almost forgotten the injustice which has been done me, and have become calm after the first burst of indignation has passed. But what would be the thoughts of these people if in the meantime they were summoned to their last account, and were found without the garment of charity, and were asked, "*How come you in hither, not having on a wedding garment?*" † Would they not be struck dumb with amazement as our Lord pronounces sentence upon them : "*Bind him hand and feet, and cast him into the exterior darkness: there shall be weeping and gnashing of teeth.*" ‡ Act rather with prudence now, and imitate the conduct of Christ, Who prayed to His Father, "*Father, forgive them,*" at the moment when He was the object of their scoffs, when the blood was trickling drop by drop from His hands and feet, and His whole body was the prey of exquisite tortures. He is the true and only Master, to Whose voice all should listen who would not be led into error: to Him did the Eternal Father refer when a voice was heard from heaven saying, "*Hear ye Him.*"§ In Him are "*all the treasures of the wisdom and of the knowledge*" of GOD.‖ If you could have asked the opinion of Solomon on any point, you might with safety have followed his advice; but "*behold a greater than Solomon here.*" ¶

Still I hear some further objecting. If we resolve to

* 1 Cor. iv. 12, 13.   † St. Matt. xii. 12.   ‡ St. Matt. xxi. 13.
§ St. Matt. xvii. 5.   ‖ Coloss. ii. 3.   ¶ St. Matt. xii. 42.

return good for evil, a kindness for an insult, a blessing for a curse, the wicked will become insolent, scoundrels will become bold, the just will be oppressed, and virtue will be trodden under foot. This result will not follow, for often, as the Wise Man says, "*A mild answer breaketh wrath.*" * Besides, the patience of a just man not unfrequently fills his oppressor with admiration, and persuades him to proffer the hand of friendship. Moreover, we forget that the State appoints magistrates, kings, and princes, whose duty it is to make the wicked feel the severity of the law, and provide means for honest men to live a peaceful and quiet life. And if in some cases human justice is tardy, the providence of GOD, which never allows a wicked act to go unpunished or a good deed to pass unrewarded, is continually watching over us, and is taking care in an unforseen way that the occurrences which evil men think will crush them shall tend to the exaltation and the honour of the virtuous. So at least St. Leo says, "Thou hast been furious, O persecutor of the Church of GOD ; thou hast been furious with the martyr, and thou hast augmented his glory by increasing his pain. For what has thy ingenuity devised which has not turned to his honour when even the very instruments of his torture have been carried in triumph." The same may be said of all martyrs, as well as of the saints of the old law. For what brought more renown and glory to the Patriarch Joseph than the persecution of his brethren. Their selling him in their envy to the Ishmaelites was the occasion of his becoming lord of the whole of Egypt, and prince of all his brothers.

But omitting these considerations, we will pass in review the many and great inconveniences those men suffer who, to escape merely a shadow of dishonour before men, are obstinately determined to have their revenge on

* Prov. xv. 1.

those who have done them any wrong. In the first place, they act the part of fools by preferring a greater evil to a lesser. For it is a principle acknowledged on all sides, and declared to us by the Apostle in these words: "*Let us not do evil that there may come good.*"* It follows by consequence, that a greater evil is not to be committed in order to obtain any compensation for a lesser one. He who receives an injury receives what is called the evil of a hardship: he who avenges an injury is guilty of what is called the evil of crime. Now, beyond a doubt, the misfortune of committing a crime is greater than the misfortune of having to endure a hardship; for though a hardship may make a man miserable it does not necessarily make him wicked; a crime however makes him both miserable and wicked: a hardship deprives a man of a temporal good, a crime deprives him of both a temporal and an eternal good. Accordingly he who would remedy the evil of a hardship by committing a crime is like a man who would cut off a part of his foot to make a pair of very small shoes fit him, which would be a sheer act of madness. Nobody is guilty of such folly in his temporal concerns, yet there are some men so blind to their real interests as not to fear to offend GOD mortally in order to escape that which has the appearance of disgrace, and maintain a semblance of honour in the eyes of men. For they fall under the displeasure and the wrath of GOD, and unless they amend in time and do penance, will have to endure eternal disgrace and torment, and will forfeit the everlasting honour of being a citizen of heaven. In addition to this, they perform an act most agreeable to the devil and his angels, who urge on this man to do an unjust thing to that man with the purpose of sowing discord and enmity in the world. And each one should calmly reflect how disgraceful it is to please the fiercest enemy of the human race, and to displease

* Rom. iii. 8.

Christ. Besides it occasionally happens that the injured man who longs for revenge mortally wounds his antagonist and slays him, for which murder he is ignominiously executed, and all his property is confiscated by the State, or at least he is forced to go into exile, and both he himself and all his family drag out a miserable existence. Thus it is that the devil sports with and mocks those who choose to be fettered with the manacles of a false honour rather than become the servants and friends of Christ, the best of Kings, and be reckoned as the heirs of a kingdom the most vast and the most enduring. Wherefore, since the foolish men who, in spite of the command of GOD, refuse to be reconciled with their enemies, expose themselves to such a total shipwreck, all who are wise will listen to the doctrine which Christ, the Master of all, has taught us in the Gospel by His words, and on the Cross by His deeds.

CHAPTER IV.

The literal explanation of the second word, "Amen I say to thee, this day thou shalt be with Me in Paradise."

THE second word or the second sentence pronounced by Christ on the Cross, was, according to the testimony of St. Luke, the magnificent promise He made to the thief who was hanging on a cross beside Him. The promise was made under the following circumstances. Two thieves were crucified along with our Lord, one on His right hand, the other on His left, and one of them added to his past crimes the sin of blaspheming Christ, and of taunting Him for His want of power to save them, saying—"*If Thou be Christ, save Thyself and us.*"* St. Matthew and St. Mark,

* St. Luke xxiii. 39.

indeed, accuse both the thieves of this sin, but it is more probable that the two Evangelists used the plural for the singular number, as is frequently done in the Holy Scriptures, as St. Augustine observes in his work on the Harmony of the Gospels. Thus St. Paul in his Epistle to the Hebrews, says of the Prophets: "*They stopped the mouths of lions, they were stoned, they were cut asunder, they wandered about in sheepskins and in goatskins.*"* Still there was only one Prophet, namely, Daniel, who stopped the mouths of lions; there was only one Prophet, namely, Jeremias, who was stoned, and there was only one Prophet, namely, Isaias, who was cut asunder. Moreover, neither St. Matthew nor St. Mark are so explicit on the point as St. Luke, who says most distinctly, "*And one of those robbers who were hanged, blasphemed Him.*"† However, even granted that both reviled our Lord, there is no reason why the same man should not at one moment have cursed Him, and at another have proclaimed His praises.

Nevertheless, the opinion of those who maintain that one of the blaspheming thieves was converted by Christ's prayer, "*Father, forgive them, for they know not what they do,*" is manifestly at variance with the Gospel narrative. For St. Luke says that the thief first began to blaspheme Christ after He had made this prayer; we are consequently driven to adopt the opinion of St. Augustine and St. Ambrose, who say that only one of the thieves reviled Him, whilst the other extolled and defended Him; and on this account the good thief rebuked the blasphemer: "*Neither dost thou fear God, seeing thou art under the same condemnation.*‡ Happy was the thief from his fellowship with Christ on the Cross. The rays of divine light which were beginning to penetrate the darkness of his soul, made him eager to rebuke the companion of his

---

* Heb. xii. 33—37.   † St. Luke xxiii. 39.   ‡ St. Luke xxiii. 40.

wickedness, and convert him to a better life; and this is the full meaning of his rebuke. "Thou, indeed, wishest to imitate the blasphemy of the Jews, who have not yet learnt to fear the judgments of GOD, but boast of the victory they fancy they have achieved by nailing Christ to a cross. They consider themselves free and safe and are under no apprehension of punishment. But dost not thou, who art being crucified for thy enormities, dread GOD'S avenging justice? Why addest thou sin to sin?" Then proceeding from virtue to virtue, and helped on by the increasing grace of GOD, he confesses his sins and proclaims Christ to be innocent. "*We indeed,*" he says, are "*justly,*" condemned to the death of the cross, "*for we receive the due reward of our deeds: but this Man hath done no evil.*"* Finally, the light of grace still increasing in his soul, he adds: "*Lord, remember me when Thou shalt come into Thy kingdom.*"† Admirable, indeed, was the grace of the Holy Spirit which was poured into the heart of the good thief. The Apostle St. Peter denied his Master; the thief confessed Him when He was nailed to His Cross. The disciples going to Emmaus said, "*We hoped that it was He that should have redeemed Israel.*"‡ The thief asks with confidence, "*Remember me when Thou shalt come into Thy kingdom.*" The Apostle St. Thomas declares that he will not believe in the Resurrection until he shall have beheld Christ; the thief gazing on Christ Whom he saw fastened to a gibbet, never doubts but that He will be a King after His death.

Who has instructed the thief in mysteries so profound? He calls that man Lord whom he perceives to be naked, wounded, in grief, insulted, despised, and hanging on a cross beside him: he says that after His death He will come into His kingdom. From which we may learn that the thief did not picture to himself the kingdom of Christ to

* St. Luke xxiii. 41. † St. Luke xxiii. 42. ‡ St. Luke xxiv. 21.

be a temporal one like the Jews imagined it to be, but that after His death He would be a King for ever in heaven. Who has been his instructor in secrets so sacred and sublime? No one, forsooth, unless it be the Spirit of Truth, Who awaited him with His sweetest benedictions. Christ after His Resurrection said to His Apostle: "*Ought not Christ to have suffered these things, and so enter into His glory?*"* But the thief miraculously foreknew this, and confessed Christ to be a King at the time when not a semblance of royalty surrounded Him. Kings reign during their lifetime, and when they cease to live they cease to reign; the thief, however, proclaims aloud that Christ, by means of His death would succeed to a kingdom, which is what our Lord signifies in the parable: "*A certain nobleman went into a far country to receive for himself a kingdom and to return.*"† Our Lord spoke these words a short time previous to His Passion, to show us that by His death He would go into a far country, that is, to another life; or in other words, that He would go to heaven which is far removed from the earth, to receive a great and eternal kingdom, but that He would return at the last day, and would repay every man according to his conduct in this world, either with reward or with punishment. Concerning this kingdom, therefore, which Christ would receive immediately after His death, the thief wisely said: "*Remember me when Thou shalt come into Thy kingdom.*" But it may be asked, Was not Christ our Lord a King before His death? Beyond a doubt He was, and therefore the Magi continually inquired, "*Where is He that is born King of the Jews?*"‡ And Christ Himself said to Pilate: "*Thou sayest that I am a King. For this was I born, and for this came I into the world; that I should give testimony to the truth.*"§ Yet He was a King in this world like a traveller

---

* St. Luke xxiv. 26. † St. Luke xix. 12. ‡ St. Matt. ii. 2.
§ St. John xviii. 37.

amongst strangers, therefore He was not recognized as a King except by a few, and was despised and ill-received by the majority. And so in the parable we have just quoted He said that He would go "*into a far country to receive for Himself a kingdom.*" He did not say He would *gain it* as it were from another, but would *receive it* as His own, and would return, and the thief wisely remarked, "*When Thou shalt come into Thy kingdom.*"

The kingdom of Christ is not synonymous in this passage with regal power or sway, for this He exercised from the beginning according to these verses of the Psalms. "*But I am appointed King by Him over Sion, His holy mountain.*"* "*He shall rule from sea to sea, and from the river unto the ends of the earth.*" † And Isaias says, "*A Child is born to us, and a Son is given to us, and the government is upon His shoulders.*"‡ And Jeremias, "*I will raise up to David a just branch: and a King shall reign and shall be wise, and shall execute judgment and justice in the earth.*"§ And Zacharias, "*Rejoice greatly, O daughter of Sion, shout for joy, O daughter of Jerusalem; behold thy King will come to thee, the just and Saviour; He is poor, and riding upon an ass, and upon a colt, the foal of an ass.*"|| Therefore in the parable of receiving a kingdom, Christ did not refer to sovereign power, nor indeed did the good thief in his petition, "*Remember me when Thou shalt come into Thy kingdom,*" but both spoke of that perfect bliss which delivers man from the servitude and anxiety of temporal matters, subjects him to GOD alone, to serve Whom is to reign, and by Whom he is constituted over all His works. This kingdom of unspeakable bliss of soul Christ enjoyed from the moment of His conception, but bliss of body which was His by right He did not actually enjoy until after His Resurrection. For whilst He was a

* Psalm ii. 6. † Psalm lxx. ‡ Isaias ix. 6. § Jer. xxiii. 5.
|| Zach. ix. 9.

sojourner in this vale of tears, He was subject to fatigues, to hunger and to thirst, to injuries, to wounds, and to death. But because His Body ought always to have been glorious, therefore immediately after death He entered into the enjoyment of the glory which belonged to Him; and in these terms He referred to this after His Resurrection: "*Ought not Christ to have suffered these things, and so to have entered into His glory?*" This glory He calls His own, since it is in His power to make others participators of it, and for this reason He is called the "*King of glory,*" and "*Lord of glory,*" and "*King of kings,*"* and He Himself says to His Apostles: "*I dispose to you a kingdom.*"† We, indeed, can receive glory and a kingdom, but we can bestow neither one nor the other, and we are invited to "*enter into the joy of thy Lord,*"‡ and not into our own joy. This then is the kingdom of which the good thief spoke when he said, "*When Thou shalt come into Thy kingdom.*"

But we must not pass over the many excellent virtues shadowed forth in the prayer of the holy thief. A brief review of them will prepare us for Christ's answer to the petition: "*Lord, remember me when Thou shalt come into Thy kingdom.*" In the first place he calls Him Lord, to show that he regards himself as a servant, or rather as a re-deemed slave, and acknowledges Christ to be his Redeemer. He then subjoins a simple request, but one full of faith, hope, love, devotion, and humility—"*Remember me.*" He does not say, Remember me if Thou canst: for he firmly believes Christ can do all things. He does not say, Please, Lord, remember me, for he has the fullest confidence in His charity and compassion. He does not say, I desire, Lord, to reign with you in your kingdom, for his humility forbade him. In fine, he solicits no special favour, but simply prays, "*Remember me,*" as though he would say, All

---

* Apoc. xix. 16.   † St. Luke xxii. 29.   ‡ St. Matt. xxv. 21.

I desire, Lord, is that you would deign to remember me, and cast your benignant eyes upon me, for I know that you are all-powerful and all-wise, and I put my entire trust in your goodness and love. It is clear from the concluding words of his prayer, "*When Thou shalt come into Thy kingdom,*" that he seeks nothing perishable and vain, but aspires after something eternal and sublime.

We will now give ear to the answer of Christ: "*Amen I say to thee, this day thou shalt be with Me in Paradise.*" The word *Amen* was used by Christ whenever He wished to make a solemn and serious announcement to His followers. St. Augustine has not hesitated to affirm that this word was, in the mouth of our Lord, a kind of oath. It could not indeed be an oath, according to the words of Christ: "*But I say to you not to swear at all, but let your speech be yea, yea; no, no; and that which is over and above these is evil.** We cannot, therefore, conclude that our Lord swore an oath as often as He used the word Amen. Amen was a term frequently on His lips, and sometimes he not only prefaced His remarks with Amen, but with Amen, amen. So the remark of St. Angustine that the word Amen is not an oath, but a kind of oath, is perfectly just, for the meaning of the word is truly, verily, and when Christ says: Verily I say to you, He seriously means what He says, and consequently the expression has almost the same force as an oath. With great reason, therefore, did He thus address the thief: "*Amen I say to you,*" that is, I assure you in the most solemn manner I can short of an oath; for the thief might have refused on three pleas to have given credit to the promise of Christ unless He had solemnly asseverated it. Firstly, he might have refused credence on account of his unworthiness to be the recipient of so great a reward, and so high a favour. For who could have imagined that the thief would have been

---

* St. Matt. v. 34—37.

transferred on a sudden from a cross to a kingdom? Secondly he might have refused credence by reason of the person who made the promise, seeing that He was at the moment reduced to the extreme of want, weakness, and misfortune, and the thief might thus have argued to himself: If this man cannot do a favour to His friends during his lifetime, how will He be able to assist them after His death? Lastly, he might have refused credence by reason of the promise itself. Christ promised Paradise. Now the Jews interpreted the word Paradise in reference to the body and not to the soul, since they always used it in the sense of a terrestrial Paradise. If our Lord had meant to say: This day thou shalt be with Me in a place of repose with Abraham, Isaac, and Jacob, the thief might easily have believed Him; but as He did not mean this, He therefore prefaced His promise with this assurance: "*Amen I say to you.*"

This day. He does not say I will place you on My right hand amongst the just at the Day of Judgment. Nor does He say, I will bring you to a place of rest after some years of suffering in Purgatory. Nor again, I will console you in a few months or days hence: but this very day, before the sun sets, you shall pass with Me from the gibbet of the cross to the delights of Paradise. Wonderful is the liberality of Christ: wonderful also is the good fortune of the sinner. St. Augustine, in his work on the Origin of the Soul, considers with St. Cyprian that the thief may be accounted a martyr, and that his soul went direct to heaven without passing through Purgatory. The good thief may be called a martyr because he publicly confessed Christ when not even the Apostles dared say a word in His behalf, and on account of this spontaneous confession, the death which he suffered in the company of Christ deserved as great a ward before GOD as if he had suffered it for the name of Christ. If our Lord had made no other promise than, "*Thou shalt be with Me*," this alone would have been an unspeakable blessing for the thief, since St. Augustine writes: "Where can there be anything evil with Him, and without Him where can there be anything good." Christ indeed did not make any trivial promise to those who follow Him when He said, "*If any man minister to Me, let him follow Me: and where I am there also shall My minister be.*"* To the thief, however, He promised not only His companionship, but likewise Paradise.

Although some people have disputed about the meaning of the word Paradise in this text, there seems to be no ground for the discussion. For it is certain, since it is an article of faith, that on the very day of His death the Body of Christ was placed in the sepulchre, and His soul went down into Limbo, and it is equally certain that the word Paradise, whether we talk of the celestial or terrestrial Paradise, cannot be applied either to the sepulchre or to Limbo. It cannot be applied to the sepulchre, because that was a most sorry place, the fit abode of corpses, and Christ was the only one buried in the sepulchre: the thief was buried elsewhere. Moreover, the words, "*Thou shalt be with Me*," would not have been accomplished, if Christ had spoken merely of the sepulchre. Nor can the word Paradise be applied to Limbo. For Paradise is a garden of delights, and even in the earthly paradise there were flowers and fruits, limpid waters, and a delicious mildness in the air. In the celestial Paradise there were delights without end, glory unfailing, and the seats of the blessed. But in Limbo, where the souls of the just were detained, there was no light, no cheerfulness, no pleasure; not indeed that these souls were in suffering, since the hope of their redemption and the prospect of seeing Christ was a subject of conso-

* St. John xii. 26.

lation and rejoicing to them, but they were kept like captives in prison. And in this sense the Apostle, expounding the Prophets, says, "*Ascending on high, He led captivity captive.*"* And Zacharias says, "*Thou also, by the blood of Thy testament, hast sent forth Thy prisoners out of the pit, wherein is no water,*"† where the words, "*Thy prisoners, and the pit wherein is no water,*" evidently point not to the delightfulness of Paradise but to the obscurity of a prison. Therefore in the promise of Christ the word Paradise could mean nothing else than the beatitude of the soul, which consists in the vision of GOD, and this is truly a paradise of delights, not a corporeal and a local paradise, but a spiritual and a heavenly one. For which reason, to the request of the thief, "*Remember me when Thou shalt come into Thy kingdom,*" our Lord did not reply, "*This day thou shalt be with Me*" in My kingdom, but "*Thou shalt be with Me in Paradise,*" because on that day Christ entered not into His kingdom, and did not enter it till the day of His Resurrection, when His Body became immortal, impassible, glorious, and was no longer liable to any servitude or subjection. And He will not have the good thief for His companion in this kingdom until the resurrection of all men at the last day. Nevertheless, with great truth and propriety He said to him: "*This day thou shalt be with Me in Paradise,*" since on this very day He would communicate both to the soul of the good thief and to the souls of the saints in Limbo that glory of the vision of GOD which He had received in His conception; for this is true glory and essential felicity; this is the crowning joy of the celestial Paradise. The choice of words used by Christ on this occasion is also greatly to be admired. He did not say: This day we shall be in Paradise, but, "*This day thou shalt be with Me in Paradise;*" as though He wished to explain Him-

* Ephes. iv. 8. † Zach. ix. 11.

self more fully, thus: This day thou art with Me on the Cross, but thou art not with Me in the Paradise in which I am in respect to the superior part of My Soul. But in a little while, even to-day, thou shalt be with Me not only liberated from the arms of the cross, but embraced in the bosom of Paradise.

CHAPTER V.

The first fruit to be drawn from the consideration of the second word spoken by Christ upon the Cross.

We can gather some select fruits from the second word spoken upon the Cross. The first fruit is the consideration of the immense mercy and liberality of Christ, and how good and useful a thing it is to serve Him. The many pains He was suffering might have been urged as an excuse by our Lord for not hearing the petition of the thief, but in His charity He preferred to forget His own grievous pains rather than not listen to the prayer of a poor penitent sinner. This same Lord answered not a word to the curses and reproaches of the priests and soldiers, but at the cry of a confessing sinner His charity forbade Him to be any longer silent. When He is reviled He opens not His mouth, because He is patient: when a sinner confesses His guilt, he speaks, because He is benign. But what shall we say of His liberality? Those who serve temporal masters frequently gain but a slight recompense for many labours. Even at this very day we see not a few who have spent the best years of their life in the service of princes, and retire in their old age on a small pittance. But Christ is a truly liberal Prince, a truly magnanimous Master. He receives no service at the hands of the good thief, except a few kind words and a hearty desire to assist Him, and behold with how great a reward He repays him. On this very day all the sins which he had committed during his life are forgiven: he is also ranked with the princes of his people, to wit, with the patriarchs and the prophets: and finally Christ raises him to the companionship of His table, of His dignity, of His glory, and of all His goods. "*This day,*" He says, "*thou shalt be with Me in Paradise.*" And what GOD says, He does. Nor does He defer this reward to some distant day, but on this very day He pours into his bosom "*a good measure, and pressed down, and shaken together, and running over.*"

The thief is not the only one who has experienced the liberality of Christ. The Apostles, who left either a ship, or a counting-house, or a home to serve Christ, were made by Him "*princes over all the earth,*"* and the devils, serpents, and all kinds of diseases were made subject to them. If any man has given food or clothing to the poor as an alms in the name of Christ, he shall hear these consoling words at the Day of Judgment—"*I was hungry, and you gave Me to eat; naked, and you covered Me:*"† receive, therefore, and possess My eternal kingdom. In fine, to pass over many other promises of rewards, could any man believe the almost incredible liberality of Christ, if it had not been GOD Himself Who promised that "*every one that hath left house, or brethren, or sisters, or father, or mother, or wife, or children, or lands for My name's sake, shall receive a hundred-fold, and shall possess life everlasting.*"‡ St. Jerome and other holy Doctors interpret the above-quoted text in this way. If any man, for the love of Christ, abandons anything in this present life, he shall receive a twofold reward, together with a life of incomparably more value than the trifle which he has left for Christ. In the first place, he shall receive a spiritual joy or a spiritual gift in

---

* Psalm xliv. 17.   † St. Matt. xxv. 35, 36.   ‡ St. Matt. xix. 29.

this life, a hundred times more precious than the temporal thing he forsook for Christ's sake; and a truly spiritual man would choose rather to keep this gift than exchange it for a hundred houses or fields, or other like things. Secondly, as though Almighty GOD considered this reward of little or no value, the happy merchant who barters earthly things for heavenly ones shall receive in the next world life eternal, in which one word is contained an ocean of everything good.

Such, then, is the manner in which Christ, the great King, shows His liberality to those who give themselves to His service without reserve. And are not those men foolish who, forsaking the standard of such a Monarch, desire to become the slaves of mammon, of gluttony, and of luxury? But those who know not what things Christ considers to be real riches, may say that these promises are mere words, since we often find His cherished friends to be poor, squalid, abject, and sorrowful, and on the other hand, we never behold this hundred-fold reward which is proclaimed to be so truly magnificent. So it is: the carnal man will never see the hundred-fold which Christ has promised, because he has not eyes wherewith he can see it; nor will he ever participate in that solid joy which a pure conscience and a true love of GOD begets. I will adduce, however, one example to show that even a carnal man can appreciate spiritual delights and spiritual riches. We read in a book of examples about the illustrious men of the Cistercian Order, that a certain noble and rich man, named Arnulp, left the whole of his fortune and became a Cistercian monk, under the authority of St. Bernard. GOD tried the virtue of this man by the bitter pangs of many kinds of diseases, particularly towards the end of his life; and on one occasion, when he was suffering more acutely than usual, he cried out with a loud voice: "Everything Thou hast said, O Lord JESUS, is true." Those who were present asking him what was the reason of this exclamation, he replied: "The Lord, in His Gospel, says that those who forsake their riches and all things else for His sake, shall receive a hundred-fold in this life, and afterwards life eternal. I at length understand the force and import of this promise, and I acknowledge that I am now receiving the hundred-fold for everything which I left. Indeed, the immense bitterness of this grief is so pleasing to me through the hope of the divine mercy which will be extended to me on account of my sufferings, that I would not consent to be liberated from my pains for a hundred times the value of the worldly substance I have left. For, indeed, spiritual joy which is centred in the hope of what is to come surpasses a hundred thousand times all worldly joy, which springs from the present." The reader, by pondering these words, may judge how great an esteem is to be set on the heavenly-derived virtue of the certain hope of eternal felicity.

CHAPTER VI.

The second fruit to be drawn from the consideration of the second word spoken by Christ upon the Cross.

A knowledge of the power of divine grace, and of the weakness of the human will, is the second fruit to be gathered from the consideration of the second word, and this knowledge is equivalent to saying that our best policy is to place all our confidence in the grace of GOD, and distrust entirely our own strength. If any man wishes to know the power of the grace of GOD, let him cast his eyes on the good thief. He was a notorious sinner, who had persevered in his wicked course of life to the moment when he was fastened to the cross—that is, to almost the last moment of his life; and at this critical period, when his eternal salvation was at stake, there was no one present to counsel or assist him. For although he was in close proximity to his Saviour, nevertheless he only heard the chief priests and the Pharisees declaring that he was a seducer, and an ambitious man who was aiming at sovereign power. He likewise heard his companion in wickedness taunting him in similar terms. There was no one to say one good word for Christ, and even Christ Himself did not rebut these blasphemies and maledictions. Nevertheless, by the assistance of GOD'S grace, when the gates of heaven seemed shut against him, the jaws of hell open to receive, and the sinner himself as far removed as possible from life eternal, he was suddenly illuminated from on high, his thoughts were directed into the proper channel, and he confessed Christ to be innocent and the King of the world to come, and, like a minister of GOD, rebuked his fellow-thief, persuaded him to repent, and commended himself humbly and devoutly to Christ. In a word, his dispositions were so perfect as to make the pains of his crucifixion compensate for what sufferings were in store for him in Purgatory, so that immediately after death he entered into the joy of his Lord. From which circumstance it is evident that no one should despair of salvation, since the thief who entered the Lord's vineyard almost at the twelfth hour received his reward with those who had come at the first hour. On the other hand, in order to let us see the extent of human weakness, the bad thief is not converted either by the immense charity of Christ, Who so lovingly prayed for His executioners, or by the force of his own sufferings, or by the admonition and example of his companion, or by the unusual darkness, the splitting of rocks, or the conduct of those who, after the death of Christ, returned to the city striking their breasts. And all these things took place after the conversion of the good

D

thief, to show us that whilst one could be converted without these adjuncts, the other, with all these helps, could not, or rather would not be converted.

But you may ask, why has GOD given the grace of conversion to the one and denied it to the other? I answer that both had sufficient grace given them for their conversion, and if one perished, he perished through his own fault, and if the other was converted, he was converted by the grace of GOD, though not without the cooperation of his own free will. Still it may be urged, why did not GOD give to both of them that efficacious grace which would overcome the hardest heart. The reason why He has not done so is one of those secrets which we ought to admire but not pry into, since we ought to rest satisfied with the thought that there cannot be injustice with GOD, as the Apostle says,* or, as St. Augustine expresses it, the judgments of GOD may be secret, but cannot be unjust. To learn from this example not to postpone our conversion to the approach of death, is a lesson that more nearly concerns us. For if one thief cooperated with the grace of GOD in that last moment, the other rejected it, and met his final doom. And every reader of history, or observer of what takes place around him, cannot but know that the rule is for men to end a wicked life by a miserable death, whilst it is the exception for the sinner to die happily; and, on the other hand, it seldom happens that those who live well and holily come to a sad and miserable end, but many good and pious people enter, after their death, into the possession of eternal joys. Those persons are too presumptuous and fool-hardy who, in a matter of such import as eternal felicity or eternal torment, dare to remain in the state of mortal sin even for a day, seeing that they may be surprised by death at any moment, and after death there is no place for repentance, and out of hell there is no redemption.

* Rom. ix. 14.

Chapter VII.

The third fruit to be drawn from the consideration of the second word spoken by Christ upon the Cross.

A third fruit can be drawn from the second word of our Lord by adverting to the fact that there were three persons crucified at the same place and at the same time, one of whom, namely, Christ, was innocent; another, namely, the good thief, was a penitent; and the third, namely, the bad thief, remained obstinate in his sin: or to express the same idea in different words, of the three who were crucified at the same time, Christ was always and transcendently holy, one of the thieves was always and notably wicked, and the other thief was formerly a sinner but now a saint. From which circumstance we are to infer that every man in this world has his cross and that those who seek to live without having a cross to carry, aim at something which is impossible, whilst we should hold those persons to be wise who receive their cross from the hand of the Lord, and bear it even to death, not only patiently but cheerfully. And that each pious soul has a cross to carry can be deduced from these words of our Lord: "*If any man will come after Me, let him deny himself, and take up his cross, and follow Me:*"* and again, "*Whosoever doth not carry his cross and come after Me cannot be My disciple,*"† which is precisely the doctrine of the Apostle: "*All that will live godly,*" he says, "*in Christ Jesus shall suffer persecution.*"‡ The Greek and Latin Fathers give their entire adhesion to this teaching, and that I may not be prolix I will give but two quotations. St. Augustine in his commentary on the Psalms writes: "This short life is a tribulation: if it is not a tribulation it is not a journey: but if it is a journey you

---
* St. Matt. xvi. 24.   † St. Luke, xiv. 27.   ‡ 2 Tim. iii. 12.

either do not love the country towards which you are journeying, or without doubt you would be in tribulation." And in another place: "If you say you have not yet suffered anything, then you have not begun to be a Christian." St. John Chrysostom, in one of his homilies to the people of Antioch, says, "Tribulation is a chain which cannot be unlinked from the life of a Christian." And again: "You cannot say that that man is holy who has not made trial of tribulation." Indeed this doctrine can be demonstrated by reason. Things of a contrary nature cannot be brought into each other's presence without a mutual opposition; thus fire and water, as long as they are kept apart, will remain quiet; but bring them together, and the water will begin to hiss, to form itself into globules, and pass off into steam until either the water is consumed, or the fire is extinguished. "*Good is set against evil,*" says Ecclesiasticus, "*and life against death: so also is the sinner against a just man.*" Just men are compared to fire. Their light is shining, their zeal is burning, they are ever ascending from virtue to virtue, ever working, and whatever they undertake they efficaciously accomplish. On the other hand sinners are compared to water. They are cold, ever moving on the earth, and forming mire on all sides. Is it therefore strange that wicked men should persecute just souls? But because, even to the end of the world, wheat and cockle will grow in the same field, chaff and corn be collected in the same barn, good and bad fish found in the same net, that is, upright and wicked men in the same world, and even in the same Church; it therefore necessarily follows that the good and the holy shall be persecuted by the bad and the impious.

The wicked also have there crosses in this world. For although they are not persecuted by the good, nevertheless they will be tormented by other sinners, by their own vices, and by their evil consciences. The most wise Solomon, who certainly would have been happy in this world, had happiness been possible here, acknowledged that he had a cross to carry when he said : "*I saw in all things vanity and vexation of mind, and therefore I was weary of my life, when I saw that all things under the sun are evil, and all vanity and vexation of spirit.*"* And the writer of the Book of Ecclesiasticus, who was likewise a most prudent man, pronounces this general sentence: "*Great labour is created for all men, and a heavy yoke is upon the children of Adam.*† St. Augustine in his commentary on the Psalms says, that "the greatest of all tribulations is a guilty conscience." St. John Chrysostom in his homily on Lazarus shows at length how the wicked must have their crosses. If they are poor, their poverty is their cross; if they are not poor, cupidity is their cross, which is a heavier one than poverty; if they are stretched on a bed of sickness, the bed is their cross; if they are not sick, they are inflamed with anger, and anger is their cross. St. Cyprian tells us that every man from the moment of his nativity is destined to carry a cross and suffer tribulation, which is foreshadowed by the tears shed by every infant. "Each one of us," he writes, "at his birth, and at his very entrance into the world, sheds tears. And although we are then unconscious and ignorant of everything, we nevertheless know, even at our nativity, what it is to cry: by a natural foresight we lament the anxieties and labours of the life we are commencing, and the untutored soul by its moaning and weeping proclaims the bustling commotions of the world which it is entering."

Since such is the case there can be no doubt but that a cross is in store for the good as well as for the wicked, and it only remains for me to prove that the cross of a saint lasts for a short time, is light and fruitful, whilst that of

* Eccles. ii. 11, 17.   † Ecclus. xl. 1.

a sinner is eternal, heavy, and sterile. In the first place there can be no question as to the fact that a saint suffers for a brief period only, since he can endure nothing when this life has passed. "*From henceforth now, said the Spirit,*" to the departing just souls, "*that they may rest from their labours;*"* "*And God shall wipe away all tears from their eyes.*"† The sacred Scriptures say most positively, that our present life is short, although to us it may appear long. "*The days of man are short,*"‡ and "*Man born of a woman, living for a short time,*" § and "*What is your life? It is a vapour which appeareth for a little while, and afterwards shall vanish away.*"‖ The Apostle, however, who carried a most heavy cross from his youth even to his old age, writes in these terms in his Epistle to the Corinthians, "*For that which is at present momentary and light of our tribulation, worketh for us above measure exceedingly an eternal weight of glory;*"¶ in which passage he speaks of his sufferings as of no account, and compares them to an indivisible moment, although they had extended over a period of more than thirty years. And his sufferings consisted in being hungry, thirsty, naked, struck, in being thrice beaten with rods by the Romans, five times scourged by the Jews, once stoned, and thrice shipwrecked; in undergoing many journeys, in being often imprisoned, in receiving stripes beyond measure, in being frequently reduced to the last extremity.** What tribulations then would he call heavy if he considers these light, as they really are. And what will you, kind reader, say, if I insist that the cross of the just is not only light, but even sweet and agreeable on account of the superabundant consolations of the Holy Spirit? Christ says of His yoke, which may be called

---

* Apoc. xiv. 13. † Apoc. xxi. 4. ‡ Job xiv. 5.
§ Job xiv. 1. ‖ St. James iv. 15. ¶ 2 Cor. iv. 17.
** 2 Cor. xi. 24.

a cross: "*My yoke is sweet and My burden light:*"* and elsewhere He says, "*You shall lament and weep, but the world shall rejoice, and you shall be made sorrowful, but your sorrow shall be turned into joy.*"† And the Apostle writes: "*I am filled with comfort; I exceedingly abound with joy in all our tribulation.*"‡ In a word, we cannot deny but that the cross of the just is not only light and temporary, but fruitful, useful, and the bearer of every good gift, when we hear our Lord saying: "*Blessed are they that suffer persecution for justice' sake, for theirs is the kingdom of heaven.*"§ St. Paul, exclaiming that, "*The sufferings of this time are not worthy to be compared with the glory to come, that shall be revealed in us,*"‖ and St. Peter exhorting us to rejoice if "*we partake of the suffering of Christ, that when His glory shall be revealed we may also be glad with exceeding joy.*"¶

On the other hand there is no need of a demonstration to show that the cross of the wicked is eternal in its duration, most heavy and unmeritorious. Of a surety the death of the wicked thief was not a descent from the cross, as the death of the good thief was, for even now that wretched man is dwelling in hell, and will dwell there for ever, since "*the worm,*" of the wicked, "*shall not die, and the fire of hell shall not be quenched.*"** And the cross of the rich glutton, that is, the cross of those who store up riches, which are most aptly compared by our Lord to thorns that cannot be handled or kept with impunity, does not cease with this life as the cross of poor Lazarus did, but it accompanies him to hell where it unceasingly burns and torments him, and forces him to cry out for a drop of water to cool his burning tongue "*for I am tormented in this flame.*"†† Therefore the

---

* St. Matt. xi. 30. † St. John xvi. 20. ‡ 2 Cor. vii. 4.
§ St. Matt. v. 10. ‖ Rom. viii. 18. ¶ 1 St. Peter iv. 13.
** Isaias lxvi. 24. †† St. Luke xvi. 24.

cross of the wicked is eternal in its duration, and the lamentations of those of whom we read in the book of Wisdom, testify that it is heavy and rough. "*We wearied ourselves in the way of iniquity and destruction, and have walked through hard ways.*"* What! are not ambition, avarice, luxury, difficult paths to tread? Are not the accompaniments of these vices, anger, quarrelling, envy, difficult paths to tread? Are not the sins which springs from these accompaniments, treachery, brawls, affronts, wounds and murder, difficult paths to tread? They are certainly such, and not unfrequently force men to commit suicide in despair, and thereby seeking to avoid one cross, prepare for themselves a much heavier one.

And what advantage or fruit do the wicked derive from their cross? It can no more bring them an advantage than thorns can produce grapes, or thistles figs. The yoke of our Lord brings peace, according to His own words: "*Take up My yoke upon you, and you shall find rest to your souls.*"† Can the yoke of the devil, which is diametrically opposed to that of Christ, bring anything but care and anxiety? And this is of still greater importance, that whereas the Cross of Christ is the step to eternal felicity, "*for it behoveth Christ to suffer and so to enter into His glory,*"‡ the cross of the devil is the step to eternal torments, according to the sentence pronounced on the wicked: "*Depart from Me, you cursed, into everlasting fire, which was prepared for the devil and his angels.*"§ If there be any wise men who are crucified in Christ, they will not seek to come down from the cross, as the impenitent thief foolishly sought, but will rather remain close to His side with the good thief, and will ask pardon of GOD and not a deliverance from the cross, and thus suffering alone with Him they will likewise

* Wisdom v. 7.
† St. Matt. xi. 29.   ‡ St. Luke xxiv. 26.   § St. Matt. xxv. 41.

reign with Him, according to the words of the Apostle: *"Yet so if we suffer with Him, that we may be also glorified with Him."** If, however, there be any wise amongst those who are weighed down by the devil's cross, they will take care to shake it off at once, and if they have any sense will exchange the five yoke of oxen for the single yoke of Christ. By the five yoke of oxen are meant the labours and uneasiness of sinners who are the slaves of their five senses; and when a man labours in doing penance instead of sinning, he barters the five yoke of oxen for the single yoke of Christ. Happy is the soul which knows how to crucify the flesh with its vices and concupiscences, and distributes the alms which might be spent in gratifying its passions, and spends in prayer and spiritual reading, in soliciting the grace of GOD and the patronage of the Heavenly Court the hours which might be lost in banqueting and in satisfying the restless ambition of becoming the friends of the powerful. In this manner the cross of the bad thief, which is heavy and barren, may be profitably exchanged for the Cross of Christ, which is light and fruitful.

We read in St. Austin how a distinguished soldier argued with one of his comrades about taking up the Cross. "Tell me, I pray, to what goal will all the labours we undertake bring us? What object do we present to ourselves? For whose sake do we serve as soldiers? Our greatest ambition is to become the friends of the Emperor; and is not the road that leads us to his honour full of dangers, and when we have gained our point, are we not then placed in the most perilous position of all. And through how many years shall we have to labour to secure this honour. But if I desire to become the friend of GOD, I can become His friend at this moment." Thus he argued, that since to secure the friendship of the Emperor

* Rom. viii. 17.

he must undertake many long and fruitless toils, he would be acting more wisely if he undertook fewer and lighter and more useful labours to secure the friendship of GOD. Both soldiers made their resolve on the spot, both left the army in order to serve their Creator in earnest, and what increased their joy on taking this step was the fact that the two ladies whom they were on the point of marrying spontaneously offered their virginity to GOD.

CHAPTER VIII.

The literal explanation of the third word—" Behold thy Mother: Behold thy son."

The last of the three words, which have special reference to charity for one's neighbour, is, *" Behold thy Mother: Behold thy son."** But before we explain the meaning of this word we must dwell a little on the preceding passage of St. John's Gospel. *" Now there stood by the Cross of Jesus His Mother, and His Mother's sister, Mary, the wife of Cleophas, and Mary Magdalene. When Jesus, therefore, saw His Mother, and the disciple standing by, whom He loved, He saith unto His Mother: Woman, behold thy son! Then saith He to the disciple: Behold thy Mother! And from that hour that disciple took her unto his own home."* Two of the three Marys that stood near the Cross are known, namely, MARY, the Mother of our Lord, and Mary Magdalene. About Mary, the wife of Cleophas, there is some doubt; some suppose her to have been the daughter of St. Ann, who had three daughters, to wit, MARY, the Mother of Christ, Mary,

* St. John xix. 26, 27.

the wife of Cleophas, and Mary Salome. But this opinion is almost exploded. For, in the first place, we cannot suppose three sisters to be called by the same name. Moreover, we know that many pious and erudite men maintain that our Blessed Lady was St. Ann's only child; and there is no other Mary Salome mentioned in the Gospels. For where St. Mark* says that "*Mary Magdalene, and Mary, the mother of James and Salome, had brought sweet spices,*" the word Salome is not in the genitive case, as if he wished to say Mary, the mother of Salome, as just before he said Mary, the mother of James, but it is of the nominative case and of the femine gender, as is clear from the Greek version, where the word is written Σαλώμη. Moreover, this Mary Salome was the wife of Zebedee,† and the mother of the Apostles, St. James and St. John, as we learn from the two Evangelists, St. Matthew and St. Mark,‡ just as Mary, the mother of James was the wife of Cleophas, and the mother of St. James the Less and St. Jude. Wherefore the true interpretation is this, that Mary, the wife of Cleophas, was called the sister of the Blessed Virgin because Cleophas was the brother of St. Joseph, the Spouse of the Blessed Virgin, and the wives of two brothers have a right to call themselves and be called sisters. For the same reason St. James the Less is called the brother of our Lord, although he was only His cousin, since he was the son of Cleophas, who, we have said, was the brother of St. Joseph. Eusebius gives us this account in his Ecclesiastical history, and he quotes, as a trustworthy authority, Hegesippus, a cotemporary of the Apostles. We have also St. Jerome's authority for the same interpretation, as we may gather from his work against Helvidius.

There is also an apparent discongruity in the Gospel

---

* St. Mark xvi. 1.
† St. Matt. xxvii. 56.   ‡ St. Mark xv. 40.

narratives, which it would be well briefly to dwell upon. St. John says that these three women stood near the Cross of the Lord, whereas both St. Mark* and St. Luke† say they were afar off. St. Austin in his third book on the Harmony of the Gospels, makes the three texts harmonize in this way. These holy women may be said to have been both a long way from the Cross, and near the Cross. They were a long way from the Cross in reference to the soldiers and executioners, who were in such close proxmity to the Cross as to touch it, but they were sufficiently near the Cross to hear the words of our Lord, which the crowd of spectators, who were the furthest of all removed, could not hear. We may also explain the texts thus. During the actual nailing of our Lord to the Cross, the concourse of soldiers and people kept the holy women at a distance, but as soon as the Cross was fixed in the ground many of the Jews returned to the city, and then the three women and St. John drew nearer. This explanation does away with the difficulty as to the reason why the Blessed Virgin and St. John applied to themselves the words, "*Behold thy son: Behold thy Mother,*" when so many others were present, and Christ addressed neither His Mother nor His disciple by name. The real answer to this objection is that the three women and St. John were standing so near the Cross as to enable our Lord to designate by His looks the persons whom He was addressing. Besides, the words were evidently spoken to His personal friends, and not to strangers. And amongst His personal friends who were on the spot there was no other man to whom He could say, "*Behold thy Mother,*" except St. John, and there was no other woman who would be rendered childless by His death except His Virgin Mother. Wherefore He said to His Mother: "*Behold thy son,*" and to His disciple, "*Behold*

---

* St. Mark xv. 40 † St. Luke xxiii. 49.

thy Mother." Now this is the literal meaning of these words: I indeed am on the point of passing from this world to the bosom of My Heavenly Father, and since I am fully aware that you My Mother, have neither parents, nor a husband, nor brothers, nor sisters, in order not to leave you utterly destitute of human succour, I commend you to the care of My most beloved disciple John: he will act towards you as a son, and you will act towards him as a mother. And this counsel or command of Christ, which showed Him to be so mindful of others, was alike welcome to both parties, and both we may believe to have bowed their heads in token of their acquiescence, for St. John says of himself: "*And from that hour that disciple took her unto his own home,*" that is, he immediately obeyed our Lord, and reckoned the Blessed Virgin, together with his now aged parents Zebedee and Salome amongst the persons for whom it was his duty to care and provide.

There still remains another question which may be asked. St. John was one of those who had said:* "*Behold we have forsaken all, and followed Thee; what shall we have therefore?*" And among the things which they had abandoned, our Lord enumerates father and mother, brothers and sisters, house and lands; and St. Matthew, when speaking of St. John and his brother St. James, said: "*And they immediately left their nets and their father and followed Him.*" † Whence comes it then that he who had left one mother for the sake of Christ, should be told by our Lord to look upon the Blessed Virgin in the light of a mother? We have not far to go for an answer. When the Apostles followed Christ they left their father and mother, inasmuch as they might be an impediment to their evangelical life, and, inasmuch as any worldly advantage and carnal pleasure might be derived from

* St. Matt. xix. 27. † St. Matt. iv. 22.

their presence. But they did not forego that solicitude which a man is justly bound to show for his parents or his children, if they want either his direction or his assistance. Whence some spiritual writers affirm that that son cannot enter a religious order, whose father is either so stricken with age, or oppressed with poverty as to be unable to live without his aid. And as St. John left his father and mother when they stood not in need of him, so when Christ ordered him to take care of and provide for His Virgin Mother, she was destitute of all human succour. GOD indeed, without any assistance from man, might have provided His Mother with all things necessary by the ministry of angels, just as they ministered to Christ Himself in the desert: but He wished St. John to do this in order that whilst the Apostle took care of the Virgin, she might honour and help the Apostle. For GOD sent Elias to the assistance of a poor widow, not that He could not have supported her by means of a raven, as He had done before, but in order, as St. Austin observes, that the prophet might bless her. Wherefore it pleased our Lord to intrust His Mother to the care of St. John for the twofold purpose of bestowing a blessing upon him, and to prove that he above all the rest was His beloved disciple. For truly in this transfer of His Mother was fulfilled that text: "*Every one that hath forsaken father or mother shall receive a hundredfold, and shall inherit life everlasting.*" * For certainly he received a hundredfold, who leaving his mother, the wife of a fisherman, received as a mother, the Mother of the Creator, the Queen of the world, who was full of grace, blessed among women, and shortly to be raised above all the choirs of angels in the heavenly kingdom.

* St. Matt. xix. 29.

CHAPTER IX.

The first fruit to be drawn from the consideration of the third word spoken by Christ upon the Cross.

If we examine attentively all the circumstances under which this third word was spoken, we may gather many fruits from its consideration. First of all, we have brought before us the intense desire which Christ felt of suffering for our salvation in order that our redemption might be copious and plentiful. For in order not to increase the pain and sorrow they feel, some men take measures to prevent their relatives being present at their death, particularly if their death is to be a violent one, accompanied by disgrace and infamy. But Christ was not satiated with His own most bitter Passion, so full of grief and shame, but wished also that His Mother and the disciple whom He loved, should be present, and should even stand near the Cross in order that the sight of the sufferings of those most dear to Him might augment His own grief. Four streams of blood were pouring from the mangled Body of Christ on the Cross, and He wished that four streams of tears should flow from the eyes of His Mother, of His disciple, of Mary His Mother's sister, and of Magdalene, the most cherished of the holy women, in order that the cause of His sufferings might be due less to the shedding of His own Blood, than to the copious flood of tears which the sight of His agony wrung from the hearts of those who were standing near. I imagine that I hear Christ saying to me: "*The sorrows of death surround Me,*"* for the sorrow of Simeon rends and mangles My Heart, as cruelly as it passes through the soul of My most innocent Mother. It is thus that a bitter death should separate not only the soul from the body,

---
* Psalm xvii. 5.

but a mother from a son, and such a Mother from such a Son! For this reason He said, "*Woman, behold thy son*," for His love for MARY would not permit Him at such a moment to address her by the endearing name of Mother. GOD has so loved the world as to give His only-begotten Son for its redemption, and the only-begotten Son has so loved the Father as to shed profusely His very Blood for His honour, and not satisfied with the pangs of His Passion, has endured the agonies of compassion, so that there might be a plentiful redemption for our sins. And that we may not perish but may enjoy life everlasting, the Father and the Son exhort us to the imitation of their charity by portraying it in its most exquisite beauty; and yet the heart of man still resists this so great charity, and consequently deserves rather to feel the wrath of GOD, than to taste the sweetness of His mercy, and fall into the arms of divine love. We should be indeed ungrateful, and should deserve everlasting torments, if we would not for His love endure the little purging which is necessary for our salvation, when we behold our Redeemer loving us to that extent, as to suffer for our sakes more than was necessary, to endure countless torments, and to shed every drop of His Blood, when one single drop would have been amply sufficient for our redemption. The only reason that can be assigned for our sloth and folly is, that we neither meditate on the Passion of Christ, nor consider His immense love for us with that earnestness and attention we ought to do. We content ourselves with reading the Passion hastily, or hearing it read, instead of securing fitting opportunities to penetrate ourselves with the thought of it. On that account the holy Prophet admonishes us: "*Attend and see if there be sorrow like unto my sorrow.*"* And the Apostle says: "*Consider him*

* Lament. i. 10.

that endureth such contradiction of sinners against himself, lest ye be wearied and faint in your minds."* But the time will come when our ingratitude towards GOD and listlessness in the affair of our own salvation will be a subject of sincere sorrow to us. For there are many who at the last day "*will groan for anguish of spirit,*" and will say: "*Therefore we have erred from the way of truth, and the light of justice hath not shined upon us.*"† And they will not feel this fruitless sorrow for the first time in hell, but before the Day of Judgment, when their mortal eyes shall be shut in death, and the eyes of their soul shall be opened, will they behold the truth of those things to which during their life they were wilfully blind.

CHAPTER X.

The second fruit to be drawn from the consideration of the third word spoken by Christ upon the Cross.

We may draw another fruit from the consideration of the third word spoken by Christ on the Cross from this circumstance, that there were three women who stood near the Cross of our Lord. Mary Magdalene is the representative of the penitent sinner, or of one who is making a first attempt to advance in the way of perfection. Mary the wife of Cleophas is the representative of those who have already made some advance towards perfection; and MARY the Virgin Mother of Christ is the representative of those who are perfect. We may couple St. John with our Lady, who was shortly to be, if he were not already, confirmed in grace. These were the only persons

---

* Heb. xii. 3.   † Wisdom v. 6.

who were found near the Cross, for abandoned sinners who never think of penance are far removed from the ladder of salvation, the Cross. Moreover, it was not without a purpose that these chosen souls were near the Cross, since even they were in need of the assistance of Him Who was nailed thereon. Penitents, or beginners in virtue, in order to carry on the war against their vices and concupiscences require help from Christ, their Leader, and this help to fight with the old serpent they receive in the encouragement which His example gives them, for He would not descend from the Cross until He had gained a complete victory over the devil, which is what we are taught by St. Paul in his Epistle to the Colossians: "*Blotting out the handwriting of ordinances that was against us, which was contrary to us, and took it out of the way, nailing it to His Cross; and having spoiled principalities and powers, He made a show of them openly, triumphing over them in it.*"* Mary the wife of Cleophas, and the mother of children who were called the brothers of our Lord, is the representative of those who have already made some progress on the path of perfection. These also want assistance from the Cross, lest the cares and anxieties of this world, with which they are necessarily mixed up, choke in them the good seed, and a night of labour will result in the capture of nothing. Therefore souls in this stage of perfection must still work and cast many a glance on Christ nailed to His Cross, Who was not satisfied by the great and manifold good deeds He performed during His life, but wished by means of His death to advance to the most heroic degree of virtue, for until the enemy of mankind had been thoroughly vanquished and put to flight, He would not come down from His Cross. To grow weary in the pursuit of virtue, and to cease from performing acts of virtue, are the

* Coloss. iii. 14, 15.

greatest impediments to our spiritual advancement, for as St. Bernard truly notes in his Epistle to Garinus, "not to advance in virtue is to go back;" and in this same epistle he refers to the ladder of Jacob, whereon all the angels were either ascending or descending, but none were standing still. Moreover, even the perfect who live a life of celibacy and are virgins, as were our Blessed Lady and St. John, who for this reason was the chosen Apostle of Christ, even these, I say, greatly need the assistance of Him that was crucified, since their very virtue exposes them to the danger of falling through spiritual pride, unless they are well grounded in humility. During the course of His public ministry, Christ gave us many lessons in humility, as when He said: "*Learn of Me, for I am meek and humble of heart.*"* And again: "*Sit ye down in the lowest place;*" † and: "*Every one that exalteth himself shall be humbled, and he that humbleth himself shall be exalted.*"‡ Still all His exhortations on the necessity of this virtue are not so persuasive as the example He set us on the Cross. For what greater example of humility can we conceive than that the Omnipotent should allow Himself to be bound with ropes and nailed to a Cross? And that He "*in Whom are hid all the treasures of the wisdom and knowledge of God*"§ should permit Herod and his army to treat Him as a fool and clothe Him with a white robe, and that "*He Who sitteth on the cherubim*"‖ should suffer Himself to be crucified between two thieves? Well might we say after this, that the man who should kneel before a crucifix, and should look into the interior of his own soul, and should come to the conclusion that he was not deficient in the virtue of humility, would be incapable of learning any lesson.

* St. Matt. xi. 29. † St. Luke xiv. 10. ‡ St. Luke xviii. 14.
§ Coloss. ii. 3. ‖ Psalm xcviii. 1.

CHAPTER XI.

The third fruit to be drawn from the consideration of the third word spoken by Christ upon the Cross.

We learn in the third place from the words which Christ addressed to His Mother and to His disciple from the pulpit of the Cross, what are the relative duties of parents towards their children, and of children towards their parents. We will treat in the first place of the duties which parents owe their children. Christian parents should love their children, but in such a manner that the love of their children should not interfere with their love of GOD. This is the doctrine that our Lord lays down in the Gospel: "*He that loveth son or daughter more than Me is not worthy of Me.*"* It was in obedience to this law that our Lady stood near the Cross to her intense agony, yet with great constancy of soul. Her grief was a proof of the great love she bore her Son, Who was dying on the Cross beside her, and her constancy was a proof of her subservience to the GOD Who was reigning in heaven. The sight of her innocent Son, Whom she passionately loved, dying in the midst of such torments, was enough to break her heart; but even had she been able, she would not have hindered the crucifixion, since she knew that all these sufferings were being inflicted on her Son according to "*the determinate counsel and foreknowledge of God.*"† Love is the measure of grief, and because this Virgin Mother loved much, therefore was she afflicted beyond measure at beholding her Son so cruelly tortured. And how could this Virgin Mother help loving her Son, when she knew that He excelled the rest of mankind in every kind of excellence, and when He was related to her by a closer tie than other children are

* St. Matt. x. 37.   † Acts ii. 23.

related to their parents? There is a twofold reason why parents love their offspring; one, because they have begotten them, and the other, because the good qualities of their children redound on themselves. There are some parents, however, who feel but a slight attachment to their children, and others who positively hate them if they are deformed or wicked, or have the misfortune of being illegitimate. Now for the aforesaid twofold reason, the Virgin Mother of GOD loved her Son more than any other mother could love her child. In the first place, no woman has ever given birth to a child without the cooperation of her husband, but the Blessed Virgin brought forth her Son without any contact with man; as a Virgin she conceived Him, and as a Virgin she brought Him forth, and as Christ our Lord in the divine generation has a Father without a Mother, so in the human generation He has a Mother without a Father. When we say that Christ our Lord was conceived of the Holy Ghost, we do not mean that the Holy Spirit is the Father of Christ, but that He formed and moulded the Body of Christ, not out of His own substance, but from the pure flesh of the Virgin. Truly then has the Virgin alone begotten Him, she alone can claim Him as her own Son, and therefore has she loved Him with more than a mother's love. In the second place, the Son of the Virgin not only was and is beautiful beyond the children of men, but is extolled alike by angels and by men, and as a natural consequence of her great love, the Blessed Virgin mourned over the Passion and death of her Son more than others, and St. Bernard does not hesitate to affirm in one of his sermons, that the sorrow our Lady felt at the crucifixion was a martyrdom of the heart, according to the prophecy of Simeon: "*A sword shall pierce through thy own soul.*"*
And since the martyrdom of the heart is more bitter than

---
* St. Luke ii. 35.

the martyrdom of the body, St. Anselm in his work on the *Excellence of the Virgin*, says that the grief of the Virgin was more bitter than any bodily suffering. Our Lord, in His Agony in the Garden of Gethsemani, suffered a martyrdom of the heart by passing in review all the sufferings and torments He was to endure on the morrow, and by opening on to His soul the floodgates of grief and fear He began to be so afflicted, that a sweat of blood diffused from His Body, an occurrence which we are not informed ever resulted from His corporal sufferings. Therefore, beyond a doubt, our Blessed Lady carried a most heavy cross, and endured most poignant grief, from the sword of sorrow which pierced her soul, but she stood near the Cross the very model of patience, and beheld all His sufferings without manifesting a sign of impatience, because she sought the honour and glory of GOD rather than the gratification of her maternal love. She did not fall to the ground half dead with sorrow, as some imagine; nor did she tear her hair, nor sob and cry aloud, but she bravely bore the affliction which it was the will of GOD she should bear. She loved her Son vehemently, but she loved the honour of GOD the Father and the salvation of mankind more, just as her Divine Son preferred these two objects to the preservation of His life. Moreover, her unwavering faith in the Resurrection of her Son increased her confidence of soul to such an extent that she stood in no need of consolation from any man. She was aware that the death of her Son would be like a short sleep, according to what the royal psalmist had said: "*I have slept and have taken my rest, and I have risen up, because the Lord hath protected me.*"*

All the faithful should imitate this example of Christ by deferring the love of their children to the love of GOD, Who is the Father of all, and loves all with a greater and

* Psalm iii. 6.

more beneficial love than we can bear ourselves. In the first place, Christian parents should love their children with a manly and prudent love, not encouraging them if they do wrong, but educating them in the fear of GOD, and correcting them, even chastising and punishing them if they either offend GOD or neglect their studies. For this is the will of GOD, as it is revealed to us in Holy Writ, in the Book of Ecclesiasticus, "*Hast thou children? instruct them, and bow down their neck from their childhood.*"* And we read of Tobias that "*from his infancy he taught his son to fear God and to abstain from all sin.*"† The Apostle warns parents not to provoke their children to anger, lest they be discouraged, but to bring them up in the nurture and admonition of the Lord, that is, to treat them not as slaves, but as children.‡ Parents who are too severe with their children, and who rebuke and punish them even for a small fault, treat them as slaves, and such treatment will discourage them and make them hate the paternal roof; and on the contrary, those parents who are too indulgent will rear up immoral children, who will become victims of hell-fire instead of possessing an immortal crown in heaven.

The right method for parents to adopt in the education of their children is to teach them to obey their superiors, and when they are disobedient to correct them, but in such a manner as to make it evident that the correction proceeds from a spirit of love and not of hatred. Moreover, if GOD calls a child to the priesthood or to the religious life, no impediment should be offered to his vocation, for parents should not oppose the will of GOD, but should say with holy Job: "*The Lord gave, and the Lord hath taken away: blessed be the name of the Lord.*"§ Lastly, if parents lose their children by an untimely death,

---

* Ecclus. vii. 24. † Tobias i. 10. ‡ Coloss. iii. 21; Ephes. vi. 4.
§ Job i. 21.

as our Blessed Lady lost her Divine Son, they should trust in the good judgment of GOD, who sometimes takes a soul to Himself if He perceives that it may lose its innocence and so perish for ever. Truly if parents could penetrate into the designs of GOD in the death of a child, they would rejoice rather than weep; and if we had a lively faith in the Resurrection, as our Lady had, we should no more repine because a person dies in his youth, than we should weep because a person goes to sleep before night-time, since the death of the faithful is a kind of sleep, as the Apostle tells us in his Epistle to the Thessalonians: *"But I would not have you to be ignorant, brethren, concerning them who are asleep, that ye sorrow not, even as others who have no hope."** The Apostle speaks rather of hope than of faith, because he does not refer to an uncertain resurrection, but to a happy and glorious resurrection, similar to that of Christ, which was a waking up to true life. For the man who has a firm faith in the resurrection of the body, and trusts that his dead child will rise again to glory, has no cause for sorrow, but great reason for rejoicing, because his child's salvation is secured.

Our next point is to treat of the duty which children owe their parents. Our Lord in His Death gave us a most perfect example of filial respect. Now, according to the words of the Apostle, the duty of children is *to requite their parents.*† Children requite their parents when they provide all necessary conveniences for them in their old age, just as their parents procured food and raiment for them in their infancy. When Christ was at the point of death He entrusted His aged Mother, who had no one to care for her, to the protection of St. John, and told her to look upon him in future as her son, and commanded St. John to reverence her as his mother. And thus our Lord perfectly fulfilled the obligations which a son owes his

---

* Thess. iv. 13. † 1 Tim. v. 4.

mother. In the first place, in the person of St. John He gave His Virgin Mother a son who was of the same age as Himself, or perhaps a year younger, and therefore was in every way capable to provide for the comfort of the Mother of our Lord. Secondly, He gave her for a son the disciple whom He loved more than the rest, and who ardently returned Him love for love, and consequently our Lord had the greatest confidence in the diligence with which His disciple would support His Mother. Moreover He chose the disciple whom He knew would outlive the other apostles, and would consequently survive His parent. Lastly, our Lord was mindful of His Mother at the most calamitous moment of His life, when His whole Body was the prey of sufferings, when His whole Soul was racked by the insolent taunts of His enemies, and He had to drink the bitter chalice of approaching death, so that it would seem He could think of nothing but His own sorrows. Nevertheless, His love for His Mother triumphed over all, and forgetting Himself, His only thought was how to comfort and help her, nor was His hope in the promptitude and fidelity of His disciple deceived, for "*from that hour he took her unto his own home.*" *

Every child has a greater obligation than our Lord had to provide for the temporal wants of his parents, since every man owes more to his parents than Christ owed to His Mother. Each infant receives a greater favour from his parents than he can ever hope to repay, for he has received from their hands what it is impossible for him to bestow on them, namely, a being. "*Remember*," says Ecclesiasticus, "*that thou hadst not been born but through them.*" † Christ alone is an exception to this rule. He indeed received from His Mother His life as a man, but He bestowed on her three lives; her human

* St. John xix. 27.   † Ecclus. vii. 30.

life, when with the cooperation of the Father and the Holy Ghost He created her: her life of grace, when He forestalled her in the sweetness of His blessings by creating her Immaculate, and her life of glory when she was assumed into the kingdom of glory, and exalted above all the choirs of angels. Wherefore if Christ, Who gave His Blessed Mother more than He had received from her in His birth, wished to *requite her*, certainly the rest of mankind are still more obliged to requite their parents. Moreover, we only do our duty in honouring our parents, and yet the goodness of GOD is such as to reward us for this. In the Ten Commandments the law is laid down— "*Honour thy father and thy mother, that thou mayst be long-lived upon the land.*" * And the Holy Ghost says: "*He that honoureth his father shall have joy in his own children, and in the day of his prayer he shall be heard.*" † And GOD does not only reward those who reverence their parents, but punishes those who are disrespectful to them, for these are words of Christ: "*God hath said: He that curseth father or mother let him die the death.*" ‡ "*And he is cursed of God that angereth his mother.*" § Hence we may conclude that a parent's curse will bring ruin in its train, for GOD Himself will ratify it. This is proved by many examples; and one which St. Augustine relates in his *City of God* we will briefly narrate. In Cæsarea, a town of Cappadocia, there were ten children, namely seven boys and three girls, who were cursed by their mother, and were immediately struck by heaven with such an infliction that all their limbs shook, and in this pitiable plight, wheresoever any of them went, they were unable to bear the gaze of their fellow-citizens, and thus they wandered throughout the whole Roman world. At last two of them were cured by the relics of St. Stephen the Proto-martyr, in the presence of St. Augustine.

* Exodus xx. 12.   † Ecclus. iii. 6.   ‡ St. Matt. xv. 4.   § Ecclus. iii. 18.

CHAPTER XII.

The fourth fruit to be drawn from the consideration of the third word spoken by Christ upon the Cross.

The burden and yoke which our Lord imposed on St. John, in entrusting to his care the protection of His Virgin Mother, was indeed a yoke that was sweet, and a burden that was light. Who indeed would not esteem it a happiness to dwell under the same roof with her, who for nine months had borne in her womb the Incarnate Word, and for thirty years to enjoy the most sweet and happy communication of sentiments with her? Who does not envy the chosen disciple of our Lord, whose heart in the absence of the Son of GOD was gladdened by the constant presence of the Mother of GOD? Yet if I mistake not it is in our power to obtain by our prayers that our most kind Lord, Who became Man for our sakes and was crucified for love of us, should say to us in reference to His Mother, "*Behold thy Mother*," and should say to His Mother for each one of us: "*Behold thy son!*" Our good Lord is not avaricious of His graces, provided we approach the throne of grace with faith and confidence, with true and open but not dissembling hearts. He Who wishes to have us coheirs in the kingdom of His Father, will not disdain to have us coheirs in the love of His Mother. Nor will our most benign Lady take it amiss to have a countless host of children, since she has a heart capable of embracing us all, and ardently desires that not one of those souls should perish whom her Divine Son redeemed with His precious Blood, and His still more precious Death. Let us therefore with confidence approach the throne of the grace of Christ, and with tears humbly beg of Him to say to His Mother for each of us, "*Behold thy son*," and to us in reference to

His Mother, "*Behold thy Mother.*" How secure should we be under the protection of such a Mother! Who would dare to drag us from beneath her mantle? What temptations, what tribulation could overcome us if we confide in the protection of the Mother of GOD and of our Mother? Nor should we be the first who had secured such powerful patronage. Many have preceded us, many I say have placed themselves under the singular and maternal protection of so powerful a Virgin, and no one has been cast off by her with his soul in a perplexed and despondent state, but all who confide in the love of such a Mother are happy and contented. Of her it is written: "*She shall crush thy head.*"* Those who trust in her will safely "*walk upon the asp and the basilisk, and will trample under foot the lion and the dragon.*" † Let us, however, listen to the words of a few distinguished men out of the vast array who acknowledged that they had placed their hope of salvation in the Virgin, and to whom we may believe our Lord had said: "*Behold thy Mother,*" and of whom He had said to His Mother, "*Behold thy son.*"

The first shall be the Syrian, St. Ephrem, an ancient Father of such renown that St. Jerome informs us his works were publicly read in the churches after the Holy Scriptures. In one of his sermons on the praises of the Mother of GOD, he says: "The undefiled and pure Virgin Mother of GOD, the Queen of all, and the hope of those in despair." And again. "Thou art a harbour for those who are tossed by storms, the comfort of the world, the liberator of those in prison; thou art the mother of orphans, the redeemer of captives, the joy of the sick, and the star of safety for all." And again. "Under thy wing guard and protect me, have mercy on me who am defiled with sin. I have confidence in none other but thee, O Virgin most sincere. Hail peace, joy, and safety of the

* Gen. iii. 15. † Psalm xc. 13.

world." We will next quote St. John Damascene who was one of the first to show the greatest honour and place the greatest confidence in the protection of the most holy Virgin. He thus discourses in a sermon on the Nativity of the Blessed Virgin: "O daughter of Joachim and Anne, O Lady receive the prayers of a sinner who ardently loves and honours you, who looks up to you as his only hope of joy, as the priestess of life, and in conjunction with your Son, the leader of sinners back to grace, and the secure depositary of safety, lighten the burden of my sins, overcome my temptations, make my life pious and holy, and grant that under thy guidance I may come to the happiness of heaven." We will now select a few passages from two Latin Fathers. St. Anselm, in his work on the Excellence of the Virgin, somewhere says: " I consider it a great sign of predestination for any one to have had the favour granted him of frequently thinking of MARY." And again: "Remember that we sometimes obtain help by invoking the name of the Virgin Mother sooner than if we had invoked the name of the Lord JESUS, her only Son, and this not because she is greater and more powerful than He, nor because He is great and powerful through her, but she is so through Him. How is it then that we obtain assistance sooner by invoking her than by invoking her Son? I say that I think this is so, and my reason is that her Son is the Lord and Judge of all, and is able to discern the merits of each. Consequently when His name is invoked by any one, He may justly turn a deaf ear to the entreaty, but if the name of His Mother is invoked, even supposing that the merits of the supplicant do not entitle him to be heard, still the merits of the Mother of GOD are such that her Son cannot refuse to listen to her prayer." But St. Bernard, in language which is truly wonderful, describes on the one hand the holy and maternal affection with which the Blessed Virgin cherishes those who are devout to her, and on the other hand the tender and filial love of those who regard her as their Mother. In his second sermon on the text "*The Angel was sent*," he exclaims: "O thou, whoever thou art, that knowest thou art exposed to the dangers of the tempestuous sea of this world more than thou enjoyest the security of dry land, do not withdraw thy eyes from the splendour of this Star, from MARY the Star of the Sea, unless thou wishest to be swallowed up in the tempest. If the winds of temptations arise, if thou art thrown upon the rocks of tribulations look up to this Star, call upon MARY. If thou art tossed hither and thither on the billows of pride, ambition, detraction, or envy, look up to this Star, call on MARY. If thou art terrified at the enormity of thy crimes, perplexed at the unclean state of thy conscience, and stricken with awe for thy Judge, beginnest to be engulphed in the abyss of sadness or the pit of despair, think of MARY; in all thy dangers, in all thy difficulties, in all thy doubts think of MARY, call upon MARY. Thou wilt not go astray if thou followest her, thou wilt not despair if thou prayest to her, thou wilt not err if thou thinkest of her." The same Saint in his sermon on the Nativity of the Virgin, speaks as follows. "Raise your thoughts and judge with what affection He wishes us to honour MARY Who has filled her soul with the plentitude of His goodness, so that whatever hope, whatever grace, whatever preservation from sin is ours we may recognize as flowing from her hands." "Let us then venerate MARY with our whole hearts and all our votive offerings, for such is His will Who would have us receive everything through MARY." "My children, she is the ladder for sinners, she is my greatest confidence, she is the whole foundation of my hope." To these extracts from the writings of two holy Fathers, I will add some quotations from two holy theologians. St. Thomas, in his essay on the Angelical salutation, says: "She is blessed among women because she alone has removed the curse of Adam, brought blessings to mankind, and opened the gates of paradise. Hence she is called MARY, which name signifies 'Star of the Sea,' for as sailors steer their ship to port by watching the stars, so Christians are brought to glory by the intercession of MARY." St. Bonaventure in his *Pharetra* writes: "O most Blessed Virgin, as every one that hates you and is forgotten by you must necessarily perish, so every one that loves you and is loved by you must necessarily be saved." The same Saint in his *Life of St. Francis* speaks of that Saint's confidence in the Blessed Virgin in the following terms. "He loved the Mother of our Lord JESUS CHRIST with an unspeakable love, by her our Lord JESUS CHRIST became our brother, and by her have we obtained mercy. Next to Christ he placed all his confidence in her, he regarded her as his own and his Order's advocate, and in her honour devoutly fasted from the feast of St. Peter and St. Paul to the Assumption." With these saints we will couple the name of Pope Innocent III. who was eminently distinguished for his devotion to the Virgin, and not only extolled her in his sermons, but built a monastery in her honour, and what is more admirable, in an exhortation he made to his flock to induce them to trust in her, he used words the truth of which was afterwards exemplified in his own person. Thus he spoke in his second sermon on the Assumption: "Let the man who is sitting in the darkness of sin look up to the moon, let him invoke MARY that she may intercede with her Son, and bring him to compunction of heart. For who has ever called upon her in his distress and has not been heard?" The reader should consult cap. ix. book 2, on the *Tears of the Dove,* and see what we have there written about Pope

Innocent III. From these extracts, and from these signs of predestination, it is abundantly evident that a hearty devotion to the Virgin Mother of GOD is not a modern introduction. For it seems incredible that that man should perish in whose favour Christ had said to His Mother, "*Behold thy son,*" provided that he has not turned a deaf ear to the words which Christ had addressed to himself, "*Behold thy Mother.*"

BOOK II.

On the Last Four Words spoken on the Cross.

CHAPTER I.

The literal explanation of the fourth word, "My God, My God, why hast Thou abandoned Me?"

We have explained in the preceding Part the three first words which were spoken by our Lord from the pulpit of the Cross, about the sixth hour, soon after His crucifixion. In this Part we will explain the remaining four words, which, after the darkness and silence of three hours, this same Lord from this same pulpit proclaimed with a loud voice. But first it seems necessary briefly to explain what, and whence, and for what end arose the darkness which intervened between the three first and the four last words, for thus does St. Matthew speak: "*Now from the sixth hour there was darkness over the whole earth, until the ninth hour; and about the ninth hour Jesus cried with a loud voice, saying, Eli, Eli, lamma sabacthani? that is, My God, My God, why hast Thou forsaken Me?*"* And that this darkness arose from an eclipse of the sun is expressly told us by St. Luke: "*And the sun was darkened,*"† he says.

But here three difficulties present themselves. In the first place, an eclipse of the sun takes place at new moon, when the moon is between the earth and the sun, and this could not be at the death of Christ, because the moon was not in conjunction with the sun, as it is when there is a

---
* St. Matt. xxvii. 45, 46.   † St. Luke xxiii. 45.

new moon, but was opposite to the sun as at full moon, as the Passion occurred at the Pasch of the Jews, which, according to St. Luke, was on the fourteenth day of the lunar month. In the second place, even if the moon had been in conjunction with the sun at the time of the Passion, the darkness could not have lasted three hours, that is, from the sixth to the ninth hour, since an eclipse of the sun does not last long, particularly if it is a total eclipse, when the sun is so entirely hidden that its obscuration is called darkness. For as the moon moves quicker than the sun, according to its own proper motion, it consequently darkens the whole surface of the sun for a short time only, and, being constantly in motion, the sun, as the moon recedes, begins to give its light to the earth. Lastly, it can never happen that through the conjunction of the sun and moon the whole earth should be left in darkness. For the moon is smaller than the sun—smaller, even, than the earth, and therefore by its interposition the moon cannot so obscure the sun as to deprive the universe of its light. And if anyone should maintain the opinion that the Evangelists speak of the whole land of Palestine, and not of the whole world absolutely, he is refuted by the testimony of St. Dionysius the Areopagite, who, in his Epistle to St. Polycarp, declares that in the city of Heliopolis, in Egypt, he himself saw this eclipse of the sun, and felt this horrid darkness. And Phlegon, a Greek historian and a Gentile, refers to this eclipse when he says: "In the fourth year of the two hundred and second Olympiad, there took place a greater and more extraordinary eclipse than had ever happened before, for at the sixth hour the light of day was changed into the darkness of night, so that the stars appeared in the heavens." This historian did not write in Judæa, and he is quoted by Origen against Celsus, and Eusebius in his Chronicles for the thirty-third year of Christ. Lucian the martyr bears witness to the fact thus : " Look into our annals, and you will find that in the time of Pilate the sun disappeared, and the day was invaded by darkness." Ruffinus quotes these words of St. Lucian in the Ecclesiastical history of Eusebius, which he himself translated into Latin. Tertullian, also, in his *Apologeticon*, and Paul Orosius, in his history—all, in fact, speak of the whole globe, and not of Judæa only. Now for the solution of the difficulties. What we said above, that an eclipse of the sun happens at new moon, and not at full moon, is true when a natural eclipse takes place; but the eclipse at the death of Christ was extraordinary and unnatural, because it was the effect of the power of Him Who made the sun and the moon, the heaven and the earth. St. Dionysius, in the passage to which we have just referred, asserts that the moon at midday was seen by himself and Apollophanes to approach the sun by a rapid and unusual motion, and that the moon placed itself before the sun and remained in that position till the ninth hour, and then in the same manner returned to its own place in the east. To the objection that an eclipse of the sun could not last three hours, so that throughout that time darkness should overspread the earth, we may reply that in a natural and ordinary eclipse this would be true; this eclipse, however, was not ruled by the laws of nature, but by the will of the Almighty Creator, Who could as easily make the moon remain, as it were, stationary before the sun, moving neither quicker nor slower than the sun, as He could bring the moon in an extraordinary manner and with great velocity from its position in the east to the sun, and after three hours make it return to its proper place in the skies. Finally, an eclipse of the sun could not be perceived at the same moment in every part of the world, since the moon is smaller than the earth and much smaller than the sun. This is most true if we regard the interposition of the moon alone; but what the moon could not of itself do, the Creator of the sun and moon did, merely by not cooperating with the sun in illuminating the globe. Nor, again, can it be true, as some suppose, that this universal darkness was caused by dense and dark clouds, as it is evident, on the authority of the ancients, that during this eclipse and darkness the stars shone in heaven, and dense clouds would obscure not only the sun, but also the moon and stars.

Various are the reasons given why GOD desired this universal darkness during the Passion of Christ. There are two special ones. First, to show the very great blindness of the Jewish people, as St. Leo tells us in his tenth sermon on the Passion of our Lord, and this blindness of the Jews lasts till this moment, and will last, according to the prophecy of Isaias: "*Arise, be enlightened, O Jerusalem: for thy light is come, and the glory of the Lord is risen upon thee. For behold, darkness shall cover the earth, and a mist the people:*"* darkness, forsooth, the most dense shall cover the people of Israel, and a mist which is lighter and easily dissipated shall cover the Gentiles. The second reason, as St. Jerome teaches, was to show the enormity of the sin of the Jews. Formerly, indeed, wicked men were wont to harass, and persecute, and kill the good; now impious men have dared to persecute and crucify GOD Himself, Who had assumed our human nature. Formerly men disputed with one another; from disputes they came to oaths; from oaths to blood and slaughter; now servants and slaves have risen up against the King of men and angels, and with unheard-of audacity have nailed Him to a Cross. Therefore the whole world is filled with horror, and in order to show its detestation of such a crime, the sun has withdrawn its rays and has covered the universe with a terrible darkness.

* Isaias lx. 1, 2.

Let us now come to the interpretation of the words of our Lord: "*Eli, Eli, lamma sabacthani.*" These words are taken from the twenty-first Psalm: "*O God, my God, look upon me; why hast Thou forsaken me?*"* The words *look upon me*, which occur in the middle of the verse, were added by the Septuagint interpreters: but in the Hebrew text those words only are found which our Lord pronounced. We must remark that the Psalms were written in Hebrew, and the words spoken by Christ were partly Syriac, which was the language then in use amongst the Jews. These words: *Talitha cumi*—"*Damsel, I say to thee, Arise,*" and *Ephphetha*—"*Be thou opened*," and some other words in the Gospel are Syriac and not Hebrew. Our Lord then complains that he has been abandoned by GOD, and He complains crying out with a loud voice. Both these circumstances must be briefly explained. The abandonment of Christ by His Father might be interpreted in five ways, but there is only one true interpretation. There were indeed five unions between the Father and the Son: one the natural and eternal union of the Person of the Father with the Person of the Son in essence? the second, a new bond of union of the Divine nature with human nature in the Person of the Son, or what is the same thing, the union of the Divine Person of the Son with human nature: the third was the union of grace and will, for Christ as man was *full of grace and truth*,† as He testifies in St. John: *I do always the things that please Him:*‡ and of Him the Father spoke: "*This is My beloved Son, in Whom I am well pleased.*"§ The fourth was the union of glory, since the soul of Christ from the moment of its conception enjoyed the beatific vision: the fifth was the union of protection to which He refers when he says: "*And He that sent Me is with Me,*

* Psalm xxi. 1.
† St. John i. 14. ‡ St. John viii. 29. § St. Matth. iii. 17.

and He hath not left Me alone."* The first kind of union is inseparable and eternal, because it is founded in the Divine essence, so our Lord says : "*I and the Father are One*:"† and therefore Christ did not say : My Father, why hast Thou forsaken Me? but "*My God, why hast Thou forsaken Me?*" For the Father is called the GOD of the Son only after the Incarnation and by reason of the Incarnation. The second kind of union never has nor can be dissolved, because what GOD has once assumed He can never lay aside, and so the Apostle says : *He that spared not His own Son, but delivered Him up for us all;"*‡ and St. Peter, "*Christ suffered for us,*" and "*Christ therefore having suffered in the flesh :"*§ all which proves that it was not a mere man, but the true Son of GOD, and Christ the Lord Who was crucified. The third kind of union also still exists and ever will exist : "*Because Christ also died once for our sins, the just for the unjust,"* ‖ as St. Peter expresses it ; for the death of Christ would have profited us nothing had this union of grace been dissolved. The fourth union could not be disturbed, because the beatitude of the soul cannot be lost, since it embraces the enjoyment of every good, and the superior part of the soul of Christ was truly happy.¶

There remains then the union of protection only, which was broken for a short period, in order to allow time for the oblation of the bloody sacrifice for the redemption of mankind. GOD the Father indeed could in many ways have protected Christ, and have hindered the Passion, and for this reason in His Prayer in the Garden Christ says : "*Father, all things are possible to Thee: remove this chalice from Me, but not what I will, but what Thou wilt :"*** and again to St. Peter : "*Thinkest*

---

* St. John viii. 29.   † St. John x. 30.
‡ Romans viii. 32.   § 1 St. Peter ii. 21 ; iv. 1.   ‖ 1 St. Peter iii. 18.
¶ St. Thomas, 3. p. q. 46. art. 8.   ** St. Mark xiv. 36.

Thou that I cannot ask My Father, and He will give Me presently more than twelve legions of angels:"* Christ also as GOD could have saved His Body from suffering, for He says: "*No man taketh*" My life "*away from Me, but I lay it down of Myself;*"† and this is what Isaias had foretold: "*He was offered because it was His own will.*"‡ Finally, the blessed Soul of Christ could have transmitted to the Body the gift of impassibility and incorruption; but it was pleasing to the Father, and to the Word, and to the Holy Spirit, for the accomplishment of the decree of the Blessed Trinity, to allow the power of man to prevail for a time against Christ. For this was that hour to which Christ referred when He said to those who had come to apprehend Him: "*This is your hour and the power of darkness.*"§ Thus then GOD abandoned His Son when He allowed His human flesh to suffer such cruel torments without any consolation, and Christ crying out with a loud voice manifested this abandonment so that all might know the greatness of the price of our redemption, for up to that hour He had borne all his torments with such patience and equanimity as to appear almost bereft of the power of feeling. He did not complain of the Jews who accused Him, nor of Pilate who condemned Him, nor of the soldiers who crucified Him. He did not groan: He did not cry out: He did not give any outward sign of His suffering; and now at the point of death, in order that mankind might understand, and that we, His servants, might remember so great a grace, and value the price of our redemption, He wished publicly to declare the great suffering of His Passion. Wherefore these words: "*My God, why hast Thou abandoned Me?*" are not words of one who accuses, or who reproaches, or who complains, but, as I have said,

* St. Matt. xxvi. 53.
† St. John x. 18.   ‡ Isaias liii. 7.   § St. Luke xxii. 53.

they are the words of One Who declares the greatness of His suffering for the best of reasons, and at the most opportune of moments.

Chapter II.

The first fruit to be drawn from the consideration of the fourth word spoken by Christ upon the Cross.

We have briefly explained what has reference to the history of the fourth word: we must now gather some fruits from the tree of the Cross. The first thought that presents itself is that Christ wished to drain the chalice of His Passion even to the dregs. He remained on the Cross for three hours, from the sixth to the ninth hour. He remained for three full and entire hours, for even more than three hours, since He was fastened to the Cross before the sixth hour, and He did not die till the ninth hour, as is proved thus: The eclipse of the sun began at the sixth hour, as the three Evangelists Matthew, Mark and Luke show; St. Mark expressly says: "*And when the sixth hour was come, there was darkness over the whole earth until the ninth hour.*"* Now, our Lord uttered his three first words on the Cross before the darkness began, and consequently before the sixth hour. St. Mark explains this circumstance more clearly by saying: "*And it was the third hour, and they crucified Him;*" and by adding shortly afterwards: "*And when the sixth hour was come, there was darkness.*"† When he says that our Lord was crucified at the third hour, he means that He was nailed to the Cross before the completion of that hour, and therefore before the commencement of the sixth hour.

* St. Mark xv. 33.   † St. Mark xv. 25.

We must here notice that St. Mark speaks of the three principal hours, each of which contained three ordinary hours, just as the householder summoned workmen to his vineyard at the first, the third, the sixth, the ninth and the eleventh hours,* and as the Church calls the canonical hours Prime, Terce, Sext, Nones and Vespers, which correspond to the eleventh hour. Therefore St. Mark says that our Lord was crucified at the third hour, because the sixth hour had not yet come.

Our Lord wished then to drink the full and overflowing chalice of His Passion to teach us to love the bitter chalice of penance and labour, and not to love the cup of consolations and worldly pleasures. According to the law of flesh and the world we ought to choose small mortifications, but great indulgences; little labour, but much joy; to take a short time for our prayers, but a long time for idle conversations. Truly we know not what we ask, for the Apostle warns the Corinthians: "*And every man shall receive his own reward according to his own labour:*"† and again: "*He is not crowned unless he strive lawfully.*"‡ Eternal happiness ought to be the reward of eternal labour, but because we could never enjoy eternal happiness if our labour here was to be eternal, so our good Lord is satisfied, if during the life which passes as a shadow we strive to serve Him by the exercise of good works; besides those who spend this short life in idling, or what is still worse, in sinning and provoking their GOD to anger, are not so much children as infants who have no heart, no understanding, no judgment. "*For if Christ ought to suffer, and so to enter His glory,*"§ how can we enter into a glory which is not our own by losing our time in the pursuit of pleasures and the gratification of the flesh? If the meaning of the Gospel was obscure,

* St. Matt. xx.
† 1 Cor. iii. 8.   ‡ 2 Tim. ii. 5.   § St. Luke xxiv. 26.

and could only be understood after great labour, there might perhaps be some excuse; but its meaning has been rendered so clear by the example of the life of Him Who first preached it, that the blind cannot fail to perceive it. And not only has the teaching of Christ been exemplified by His own life, but there have been as many commentaries on His doctrine apparent to all, as there are apostles and martyrs and confessors and virgins and saints whose praises and triumphs we celebrate every day. And all these proclaim aloud that not through many pleasures, but "*through many tribulations,*" it behoveth us "*to enter into the kingdom of heaven.*"*

CHAPTER III.

The second fruit to be drawn from the consideration of the fourth word spoken by Christ upon the Cross.

Another and very profitable fruit may be gathered from the consideration of the silence of Christ during those three hours which intervened between the sixth and the ninth hour. For, O my soul, what was it thy Lord did during those three hours? Universal horror and darkness had overspread the world, and thy Lord was reposing, not on a soft bed, but on a Cross, naked, overwhelmed with sorrows, without any one to console Him. Thou, O Lord, Who alone knowest what Thou sufferedest, teach Thy servants to understand what a debt of gratitude they owe Thee, to condole with Thee with their tears, and to suffer for Thy love, if it should so please Thee, the loss of every kind of consolation in this their place of banishment.

* Acts xiv. 21.

O My son, during the whole course of My mortal life, which was nothing else but a continued labour and sorrow, I never experienced such anguish as during those three hours, nor did I ever suffer with greater willingness than then. For then through the weakness of My Body, My Wounds became every moment more open, and the bitterness of My pains increased. Then, too, the cold, which was intensified by the absence of the sun, made the sufferings from the head to the foot of My naked Body greater. Then, too, the very darkness which shut out from view the sky and the earth and all other things, forced, as it were, My thoughts to dwell on nothing but the torments of My Body, so that on this account those three hours seemed to be three years. But because My Heart was inflamed with a longing desire to honour My Father, to show My obedience to Him, and to procure the salvation of your souls, and the more the pains of My Body increased the more was this desire satiated, so these three hours seemed but three short moments, so great was My love in suffering.

O dear Lord, if such indeed was the case, we are very ungrateful if we find it hard to spend one hour in thinking of Thy pains, when Thou didst not find it hard to hang on a Cross for our salvation for three full hours, during a frightful darkness, in cold and nakedness, suffering an intolerable thirst and most bitter pangs. But, O lover of men, I beseech Thee answer me this. Could the vehemence of Thy sufferings withdraw Thy Heart from prayer for one moment during those three long and silent hours? Because when we are in distress, particularly if we suffer any bodily pain, we find the greatest difficulty in praying.

It was not so with Me, My son, because in a weak Body I had a Soul ready for prayer. Indeed during those three hours, when not a word escaped my lips, I prayed and supplicated the Father for you with My Heart. And

I prayed not with My Heart only, but also with My Wounds and with My Blood. For there were as many mouths crying out for you to the Father as there were Wounds in My Body, and My Wounds were many; and there were as many tongues beseeching and begging for you from this same Father, Who is your Father as well as Mine, as there were drops of Blood trickling to the ground.

Now at last, O Lord, Thou hast plainly confounded the impatience of Thy servant, who if perchance he comes to pray worn out with work, or weighed down with affliction, can scarcely raise up his mind to GOD to pray for himself; or if through Thy grace he does lift up his mind, he cannot keep his attention fixed, but his thoughts must wander back to his labour or his sorrow. Therefore, O Lord, have mercy on Thy servant according to Thy great mercy, that imitating the great example of Thy patience he may walk in Thy footsteps and learn to despise his slight afflictions, at least during his prayer.

CHAPTER IV.

The third fruit to be drawn from the consideration of the fourth word spoken by Christ upon the Cross.

When our Lord exclaimed on the Cross, "*My God, My God, why hast Thou forsaken Me?*" He was not ignorant of the reason why GOD had forsaken Him. For what could He be in ignorance of, Who knew all things? And thus St. Peter, when he was asked by our Lord, "*Simon, son of John, lovest thou Me?*" replied, "*Lord, Thou knowest all things: Thou knowest that I love Thee.*" *
And the Apostle St. Paul, speaking of Christ, says, "*In*

* St. John xxi. 17.

Whom are hid all the treasures of wisdom and knowledge." Christ therefore asked, not in order that He might learn anything, but to encourage us to inquire, so that by seeking and finding we might learn many things that would be useful, perhaps even necessary for us. Why, then, did GOD abandon His Son in the midst of His trials and bitter anguish? Five reasons occur to me, and these I will mention in order that those who are wiser than I may have the opportunity of investigating better and more useful ones.

The first reason that occurs to me is the greatness and the multitude of the sins which mankind have committed against their GOD, and which the Son of GOD undertook to expiate in His own Flesh: "*Who His ownself*," writes St. Peter, "*bore our sins in His Body upon the tree; that we being dead to sins, should live to justice; by Whose stripes you were healed.*"† Indeed, the enormity of the offences which Christ undertook to atone for in His Passion is in a certain sense infinite, by reason of the Person of infinite majesty and excellence which has been offended; but, on the other hand, the Person of Him Who atones, which Person is the Son of GOD, is also of infinite majesty and excellence, and consequently every suffering willingly undertaken by the Son of GOD, even if He spilt but one drop of His Blood, would be a sufficient atonement. Still it was pleasing to GOD that His Son should suffer innumerable torments, and sorrows most severe, because we had committed not one but manifold offences, and the Lamb of GOD, Who taketh away the sins of the world, took upon Himself not the sin of Adam only, but all the sins of all mankind. This is shown in that abandonment of which the Son complains to the Father: "*Why hast Thou forsaken Me?*" The second reason is the greatness and the multitude of the pains

* Coloss. ii. 3.   † 1 St. Peter ii. 24.

of hell, and the Son of GOD shows how great they are by wishing to quench them in the torrents of His Blood. The prophet Isaias teaches us how terrible they are, that they are clearly intolerable, for he asks: "*Which of you can dwell with devouring fire? Which of you shall dwell with everlasting burnings?*"* Let us therefore return thanks to GOD with our whole heart, Who was willing to abandon His only-begotten Son to the greatest torments for a time to free us from flames which would be eternal. Let us return thanks, too, from the bottom of our heart to the Lamb of GOD, Who preferred to be abandoned by GOD under His chastising sword than abandon us to the teeth of that beast who would ever gnaw and would never be satisfied with gnawing us. The third reason is the high value of the grace of GOD, which is that most precious stone which Christ, the wise merchant, purchased by the sale of everything He had, and restored to us. The grace of GOD, which had been given to us in Adam, and which we lost through Adam's sin, is so precious a stone that whilst it adorns our souls, and renders them pleasing to GOD, it is also a pledge of eternal felicity. No one could restore to us that precious stone, which was the gem of our riches, and of which the cunning of the serpent had deprived us, except the Son of GOD, Who overcame by His wisdom the wickedness of the devil, and Who gave it back to us at His own great cost, since He endured so many labours and sorrows. The dutifulness of that Son prevailed, Who took on Himself a most laborious pilgrimage to recover for us that precious gem. The fourth cause was the exceeding greatness of the kingdom of heaven, which the Son of GOD opened for us by His immense toil and suffering, and to Whom the Church gratefully sings, "*When Thou hadst overcome the sting of death, Thou didst open the kingdom of heaven*

* Isaias xxxiii. 14.

to believers." But in order to conquer the sting of death it was necessary to sustain a hard contest with death, and that the Son might triumph the more gloriously in this contest, He was abandoned by His Father. The fifth cause was the immense love which the Son had for His Father. For in the redemption of the world and in the wiping away of sin, He proposed to make an abundant and a superabundant satisfaction to the honour of His Father. And this could not have been done if the Father had not abandoned the Son, that is, had not allowed Him to suffer all the torments which could be devised by the malice of the devil, or could be endured by a man. If, therefore, any one asks why GOD abandoned His Son on the Cross when He was suffering such an extremity of torments, we can answer that He was abandoned in order to teach us the greatness of sin, the greatness of hell, the greatness of divine grace, the greatness of eternal life, and the greatness of the love which the Son of GOD had for His Father. From these reasons there arises another question: Why, forsooth, has GOD mixed the martyrs' chalice of suffering with such spiritual consolation as that they preferred to drain their chalice sweetened with these consolations, than be without the suffering and the consolation, and allowed His dearly beloved Son to drain to the dregs the bitter chalice of His suffering without any consolation? The answer is, that in the case of the martyrs none of the reasons which we have given above in reference to our Lord have any place.

CHAPTER V.

The fourth fruit to be drawn from the consideration of the fourth word spoken by Christ upon the Cross.

Another fruit may be gathered, not so much from the fourth word itself, as from the circumstances of the time in which it was spoken: that is, from the consideration of the terrible darkness that immediately preceded the speaking of the word. The consideration of this darkness would be most proper, not only for enlightening the Hebrew nation, but for strengthening Christians themselves in the faith, if they would seriously apply their minds to the force of the truths which we propose to found on it.

The first truth is that whilst Christ was on the Cross the sun was so totally obscured that the stars were as visible as they are in the night time. This fact is vouched for by five witnesses, most worthy of credibility, who were of different nations, and wrote their books both at different times and in different places, so that their writings could not have been the result of any comparison or collusion. The first is St. Matthew, a Jew, who wrote in Judæa, and was one of those who saw the sun darkened. Now certainly a man of his caution and prudence would not have written what he has written, and as is probable in the very city of Jerusalem, unless the fact he described was true. For otherwise he would have been ridiculed and laughed at by the inhabitants of the city and county for writing what everybody knew to be false. Another witness is St. Mark, who wrote at Rome; he also saw the eclipse; for he was in Judæa at the time with the other disciples of our Lord. The third is St. Luke, who was a Greek who wrote in Greece: he also saw the eclipse at Antioch.

For since Dionysius the Areopagite saw it at Heliopolis in Egypt, St. Luke could more easily see it at Antioch, which city is nearer Jerusalem than Heliopolis. The fourth and fifth witnesses are Dionysius and Apollophanes, both Greeks, and at the time Gentiles, and they distinctly assert that they saw the eclipse and were filled with astonishment at it. These are the five witnesses who bear testimony to the fact because they saw it. To their authority we may add that of the Annals of the Romans, and Phlegon, the chronicler of the Emperor Adrian, as we have shown above in the first chapter. Consequently this first truth cannot without great rashness be denied either by Jews or Pagans. Amongst Christians it is regarded as part of the Catholic faith.

The second truth is, that this eclipse could only be brought about by the almighty power of GOD: that therefore it could not be the work of the devil, or of men through the agency of the devil, but proceeded from the special providence and will of GOD, the Creator and Ruler of the world. The proof is this. The sun could only be eclipsed by one of three methods: either by the interposition of the moon between the sun and earth; or by some vast and dense cloud; or through the absorption or extinction of the sun's rays. The interposition of the moon could not by the laws of nature have happened, since it was the Pasch of the Jews, and the moon was at its full. The eclipse then must have happened either without the interposition of the moon, or the moon, by some extraordinary and great miracle, must have passed in a few hours over a space which naturally it would take fourteen days to accomplish, and then by a repetition of the miracle have returned to its proper place. Now it is admitted by everyone that GOD alone can influence the motions of the heavenly spheres, for the devils have power only in this globe, and so the Apostle calls Satan "*The prince of the power of this air.*"* The eclipse of the sun could not have happened in the second method, for a dense and thick cloud could not hide the rays of the sun without at the same time concealing the stars. And we have the authority of Phlegon for saying that during this eclipse the stars were as visible in the sky as they are during the night. As for the third method, we must remember that the rays of the sun could not be absorpt or extinguished but by the power of GOD who created the sun. Therefore this second truth is as certain as the first, and cannot be denied without an equal degree of rashness.

The third truth is that the Passion of Christ was the cause of this eclipse which was brought about by the special providence of GOD, and is proved by the fact that the darkness overshadowed the earth just as long as our Lord remained alive on the Cross, that is from the sixth to the ninth hour. This is attested by all those who speak of the eclipse; nor could it happen that an eclipse which was itself miraculous should by chance coincide with the Passion of Christ. For miracles are not the result of chance, but of the power of GOD. Nor am I aware of any author who could assign another cause for this so wonderful an eclipse. Those then that know Christ acknowledge that it was brought about for His sake, and those who do not know Him confess their ignorance of its object, but remain in admiration of the fact.

The fourth truth is, that so terrible a darkness could only show the sentence of Caiphas and Pilate to be most unjust, JESUS to be the true and only Son of GOD, the Messias promised to the Jews. This was the reason why the Jews demanded His death. For when in the council

---

* Ephes. ii. 2.

of the Priests, the Scribes, and the Pharisees, the High Priest saw that the evidence produced against Him proved nothing, he arose and said: "*I adjure Thee by the living God that Thou tell us if Thou be the Son of God.*" And on our Lord acknowledging and confessing Himself to be so, he "*rent his garments saying: He hath blasphemed, what further need have we of witnesses? Behold, now you have heard the blasphemy; what think you? But they answering said: He is guilty of death.*"* Again when He was before Pilate, who wished to liberate Him, the Chief Priests and people cried out: "*We have a law; and according to the law He ought to die, because He made Himself the Son of God.*† This was the principal reason why Christ our Lord was condemned to the death of the Cross, and it was foretold by Daniel the prophet when he said: "*Christ shall be slain: and the people that shall deny Him shall not be His.*‡ For this cause, then, during the Passion of Christ, GOD allowed a horrible darkness to overspead the world to show most clearly that the High Priest was wrong: that the Jewish people was wrong: that Herod was wrong, and that He Who was hanging on the Cross was His only Son, the promised Messiah. And when the Centurion saw these heavenly manifestations he exclaimed, "*Indeed this was the Son of God;*§ and again, "*Indeed this was a just Man.*"|| For the Centurion recognized such celestial signs as the voice of GOD annulling the sentence of Caiphas and Pilate, and declaring that this Man was condemned to death contrary to all law, since He was the author of life, the true Son of GOD, the promised Christ. For what else could GOD mean by this darkness, by the secret splitting of the rocks, and the rending of the veil of the Temple, but that He withdrew Himself from a people who were

---

* St. Matt. xxvi. 63, 65, 66.   † St. John xix. 7.   ‡ Dan. ix. 26.
§ St. Matt. xxvii. 54. || St. Luke xxiv. 47.

once His own, and was wrathful with a great wrath because they had not known the time of His visitation.

Certainly if the Jews would consider these things, and at the same time turn their attention to the fact that from that day they have been scattered through every nation, have had neither kings nor pontiffs, nor altars, nor sacrifices, nor miracles, nor prophets, they must conclude that they have been abandoned by GOD, and what is worse, have been given over to a reprobate sense, and that that is now being accomplished in them what Isaias foretold when he introduces the Lord as saying: "*Hearing hear and understand not: and see the vision and know it not. Blind the heart of this people and make their ears heavy and shut their eyes: lest they see with their eyes and hear with their ears and understand with their hearts and be converted and I heal them.*"*

CHAPTER VI.

The fifth fruit to be drawn from the consideration of the fourth word spoken by Christ upon the Cross.

In the three first words Christ our Master has recommended to us three great virtues—charity towards our enemies, kindness to those in distress, and affection for our parents. In the four last words He recommends to us four virtues, not indeed more excellent, but still not less necessary for us, humility, patience, perseverance, and obedience. Of humility, indeed, which may be called the characteristic virtue of Christ, since no mention of it has been made in the writings of the wise men of this world, He gave us examples by His actions through the whole course of His life and in chosen words showed Himself

* Isaias vi. 9, 10.

to be a Master of the virtue when He said—"*Learn of Me, because I am meek and humble of heart.*"* But at no time did He more clearly encourage us to the practice of this virtue, and along with it of patience, which cannot be separated from humility, than when He exclaimed—"*My God, My God, why hast Thou forsaken Me?*" For Christ shows us in these words that by the permission of GOD, as the darkness testified, all His glory and excellence had been obscured, and our Lord could not have borne this, had He not possessed the virtue of humility in the most heroic degree.

The glory of Christ, of which St. John writes in the beginning of his Gospel—"*We saw His glory, the glory as it were of the only-begotten Son of the Father, full of grace and truth,*"† consisted in His power, His wisdom, His uprightness, His royal Majesty, the happiness of His soul, and His divine dignity which He enjoyed as the true and real Son of GOD. The words, "*My God, My God, why hast Thou forsaken Me,*" show that His Passion threw a veil over all these gifts. His Passion threw a veil over His power, because when fastened to the Cross He appeared so powerless, that the Chief Priests, the soldiers and the thief mocked His weakness by saying—"*If Thou be the Son of God, come down from the Cross; He saved others, Himself He cannot save.*"‡ What patience, what humility was necessary for Him Who was almighty to answer never a word to such taunts. His Passion threw a veil over His wisdom, because before the High Priest, before Herod, before Pilate, He stood as one devoid of understanding and answered their questions by silence, so that "*Herod with his army set Him at nought, and mocked Him, putting on Him a white garment.*"§ What

---

* St. Matt. xi. 29.
† St. John i. 14.   ‡ St. Mark xxvii. 40—42.
§ St. Luke xxiii. 11.

patience, what humility was necessary for Him Who was not only wiser than Solomon, but was the very wisdom of GOD Himself, to tolerate such outrages. His Passion threw a veil over the uprightness of His life, since He was nailed to a Cross between two thieves, as a seducer of the people, and a usurper of another's kingdom. And Christ confessed that the being abandoned by His Father seemed to cast a greater gloom over the glory of His innocent life. "*Why hast Thou forsaken Me?*" For GOD is not wont to abandon upright, but wicked men. Every proud man indeed takes particular care to avoid saying anything which could lead his hearers to infer that he had been slighted. But humble and patient men, of whom Christ is the King, eagerly seize every occasion of practising their humility and patience, provided that in so doing there is no violation of truth. What patience, what humility was it necessary to possess, in order to endure such insults, especially for Him of Whom St. Paul says—"*It was fitting that we should have such a High Priest, holy, innocent, undefiled, separated from sinners, and made higher than the heavens.*"* His Passion cast such a veil over His regal Majesty that He had a crown of thorns for a diadem, a reed for a sceptre, a gibbet for an audience chamber, two thieves for His royal attendants. What patience then, what humility was necessary for Him Who was the true King of kings, Lord of lords, and Prince of the kings of this world. What shall I say about the happiness of soul which Christ enjoyed from the very moment of His conception, and of which, had He wished, He could have made His Body partaker. What a veil did His Passion throw over the glory of this happiness, since it made Him as Isaias says— "*Despised, and the most abject of men, a Man of sorrows, and acquainted with infirmity,*"† so that in the greatness

* Heb. vii. 26.   † Isaias liii. 3.

of His suffering He cried out, "*My God, why hast Thou forsaken Me?*" In fine, His Passion so obscured the mighty dignity of His Divine Person, that He Who is seated not only above all men, but above the very angels, could say—"*But I am a Worm and no man, the reproach of men, and the outcast of the people.*" *

Christ in His Passion, then, descended to the very abyss of humility, but this humility had its reward and its glory. What our Lord had so often promised that "*he that shall humble himself shall be exalted,*" the Apostle tells us was exemplified in His own Person. "*He humbled Himself, becoming obedient unto death, even to the death of the Cross. For which cause God also hath exalted Him, and hath given Him a name which is above all names; that in the name of Jesus every knee should bow, of those that are in heaven, on earth, and under the earth.*" † So He Who appeared to be the least of men is declared to be the first, and a short and as it were momentary humiliation has been followed by a glory which shall be eternal. Thus has it been with the Apostles and all the saints. St. Paul says of the Apostles—"*We are made as the refuse of this world, the offscouring of all even until now;*‡ that is, he compares them to the vilest things that are trodden under foot. Such was their humility. What is their glory? St. John Chrysostom tells us that the Apostles now in heaven, are seated close to the very throne of GOD, where the Cherubim praise Him and the Seraphim obey Him. They are associated with the greatest princes of the celestial court. They shall be there for ever. If men would only consider how glorious a thing it is to imitate in this life the humility of the Son of GOD, and would picture to themselves to what a height of glory this humility would lead them, we should find **very few** proud men. But since the majority of men measure

* Psalm xxi. 7. † Philip. ii. 8—10. ‡ 1 Cor. iv. 13.

everything by their senses and by human considerations, we must not be astonished if the number of the humble is small, and the number of the proud infinite.

CHAPTER VII.

The literal explanation of the fifth word, " I thirst."

The fifth word, which is found in St. John, consists of the one only word "*I thirst.*" But to understand it we must add the preceding and subsequent words of the same Evangelist. "*Afterwards Jesus knowing that all things were now accomplished, that the Scripture might be fulfilled, said, I thirst. Now there was a vessel set there full of vinegar. And they putting a sponge full of vinegar about hyssop, put it to His mouth.** The meaning of which words is, that that our Lord wished to fulfil everything, which His Prophets, inspired by the Holy Ghost, had foretold about His life and death; and now everything had been accomplished with the exception of having gall mixed with His drink, according to that of the sixty-eighth psalm: "*And they gave Me gall for My food, and in My thirst they gave Me vinegar to drink.*† Therefore was it that he cried out with a loud voice, "*I thirst;*" that the Scriptures might be fulfilled. But why in order that the Scriptures should be fulfilled? Why not rather because He was really thirsty and wished to quench His thirst? A prophet does not prophesy for the purpose of that being accomplished which he foretells, but he prophesies because he sees that that will be accomplished which he foretells, and therefore he foretells it. Consequently the foreseeing or foretelling anything is not the cause of its happening, but the event that is to happen is the cause

* St. John xix. 28, 29.   † Psalm lxviii. 22.

why it can be foreseen and foretold. Here we have a great mystery laid open before us. Our Lord had suffered a most grievous thirst from the beginning of His Crucifixion, and this thirst kept on increasing, so that it became one of the greatest pains He endured on the Cross, for the shedding a great quantity of blood parches a person, and produces a violent thirst. I myself once knew a man who was suffering from a serious wound and consequent loss of blood, who asked for nothing else but drink, as though his wound were of no consideration, but his thirst terrible. The same is related of St. Emmerammus, the martyr, who was bound to a stake, and otherwise grievously tortured, yet complained only of thirst. But Christ had been dragged backwards and forwards through the city, during the scourging at the pillar had most copiously shed that Blood which during His Crucifixion flowed from His Body, as from four fountains, and this loss of Blood had continued for hours. Must He not then have suffered a most violent thirst? Yet He endured this agony for three hours in silence, and could have endured it even to His death, which was so near at hand. Then why did He keep silent on this point for so long a time, and at the moment of death disclose his suffering by crying out, "*I thirst!*" Because it was the will of GOD that we should all know His Divine Son had suffered this agony, and so our heavenly Father had wished it to be foretold by His Prophet, and He also wished our Lord JESUS CHRIST, for the sake of giving an example of patience to His faithful followers to acknowledge that He suffered this intense agony by exclaiming, "*I thirst;*" that is, all the pores of My Body are closed, My veins are parched up, My tongue is parched, My palate is parched, My throat is parched, all My members are parched; if any one longs to relieve Me, let him give Me to drink.

Let us consider now what drink was offered Him by those who stood by the Cross. "*Now there was a vessel set there full of vinegar. And they putting a sponge full of vinegar about hyssop put it to His mouth.*" Oh, what consolation! What a relief! There was a vessel full of vinegar, a beverage which tends to make wounds smart and hasten death, and for this reason was it kept in order to make those who were crucified die the quicker. In treating of this point, St. Cyril says with truth, "Instead of a refreshing and cooling draught, they offered Him one that was hurtful and bitter." And if we consider what St. Luke writes in his Gospel, this becomes all the more probable: "*And the soldiers also mocked Him, coming to Him and offering Him vinegar.*"* Although St. Luke speaks of this as happening to our Lord as soon as He was nailed to the Cross, still we may piously believe that when the soldiers heard Him exclaiming, "*I thirst,*" they offered Him vinegar by means of that same sponge and reed which in their derision they had previously offered Him. We must conclude then that as at first a little before His Crucifixion they presented Him with wine mixed with gall, so at the point of death they gave Him vinegar, a drink most distasteful to a man in His agony, so that the Passion of Christ was from first to last a real and genuine Passion which admitted no consolation.

* St. Luke xxiv. 36.

Chapter VIII.

The first fruit to be derived from the consideration of the fifth word spoken by Christ upon the Cross.

The Scriptures of the Old Testament are often to be interpreted by the Scriptures of the New Testament, but as regards this mystery of our Lord's thirst the words of the sixty-eighth Psalm may be regarded as a commentary of the Gospel. For we cannot absolutely decide from the words of the Gospel whether those who offered our thirsting Lord vinegar did so for the purpose of affording relief, or for the sake of aggravating His pain, that is whether they did so from a motive of love or hatred. With St. Cyril we are inclined to believe that they did so in the latter sense, because the words of the Psalmist are too clear to require any explanation ; and from these words we may draw this lesson, to learn to thirst with Christ after those things, for which we may thirst with profit. This is what the Psalmist says: "*And I looked for one that would grieve together with Me, but there was none: and for one that would comfort Me, and I found none. And they gave Me gall for My food, and in My thirst they gave Me vinegar to drink.*"* And so those, who a little before His Crucifixion gave our Lord wine mixed with gall as well as those who offered our crucified Lord vinegar only, represent those of whom He complains when He says: "*I looked for one that would grieve together with Me, but there was none; and for one that would comfort me, and I found none.*"

But perhaps some one may ask : Did not His Blessed Virgin Mother, and His Mother's sister, Mary of Cleophas, and Mary Magdalene, and the Apostle St. John who stood near the Cross truly and heartily grieve together with him ?

* Psalm lxviii. 21, 22.

Did not those holy women who followed our Lord to Mount Calvary, bewailing His lot, truly grieve together with Him? Were not the Apostles, during the whole time of His Passion, in a state of sorrow, according to that prediction of Christ.—"*Amen, amen, I say to you, that you shall lament and weep, but the world shall rejoice?*"* All these grieved and truly grieved, but they did not grieve together with Christ, because the cause and reason of their sorrow was quite different from the cause and reason of Christ's sorrow. Our Lord says: "*I looked for one that would grieve together with me, but there was none, and for one that would comfort me, and I found none.*" They grieved for Christ's corporal suffering and death; but He did not grieve for this except for a short time in the garden to prove that He really was Man. Did He not say: "*With desire I have desired to eat this pasch with you before I suffer*,"† and again: "*If you loved Me, you would indeed be glad, because I go to the Father.*"‡ What then was the cause of that sorrow of our Lord in which He found none to grieve together with Him? It was the loss of souls for whom He was suffering. And what was the source of that comfort which He could find none to offer Him, but cooperating with Him for the salvation of souls after which He so ardently longed? This was the one comfort He sought after, this He desired, this He hungered for, this He thirsted for; but they give Him gall for His food, and vinegar for His drink. Sin is signified by the bitterness of the gall, than which nothing can be more bitter to one who has the sense of taste; and obstinacy in sin is shown by the sharpness and pungency of the vinegar. Christ, then, had a real cause for sorrow when He saw for the thief who was converted, not only another remain in His obstinacy but countless others besides; when

* St. John xvi. 20.
† St. Luke xxii. 15. ‡ St. John xiv. 28.

He saw that all His Apostles were scandalized at His Passion, that Peter had denied Him, that Judas had betrayed Him.

If then anyone desires to comfort and console Christ hungering and thirsting on the Cross, and full of sorrow and grief, let him in the first place show himself truly penitent; let him detest his own sins, and then along with Christ let him conceive a great sorrow in his heart, because so great a number of souls daily perish, though all could so easily be saved would they but use the grace He has purchased for them in redeeming them. St. Paul was one of those who grieved together with Christ, when in his Epistle to the Romans he says: "*I speak the truth in Christ, I lie not, my conscience bearing me witness in the Holy Ghost that I have great sadness and continual sorrow in my heart. For I wished myself to be an anathema from Christ, for my brethren, who are my kinsmen according to the flesh, who are Israelites, to whom belongeth the adoption as of children,*" &c.* The Apostle could not more closely show his longing desire for the salvation of souls than by this climax: "*For I wished myself to be an anathema from Christ.*" He means according to what St. John Chrysostom says in his work on Compunction of Heart, that he was so exceedingly afflicted at the damnation of the Jews as to wish, if it were possible, to be separated from Christ, for the sake of the glory of Christ.† He did not desire to be separated from the love of Christ, as that would be contradictory to what he elsewhere states in the same epistle: "*Who then shall separate us from the love of Christ?*"‡ but from the glory of Christ, preferring to be deprived of a participation in the glory of his Saviour rather than that his Lord should be deprived of the additional fruit of His Passion, which would accrue from the conversion of so

---
* Romans ix. 1, 2, 3.
† Lib. i. hom. 18. ‡ Rom. viii. 35.

many thousands of Jews. He truly grieved together with Christ and solaced the grief of his Divine Master. But how few imitators has the great Apostle now-a-days? In the first place, many pastors of souls are more afflicted if the revenues of the Church are diminished or lost than if a great number of souls perished through their absence or neglect. "We bear," says St. Bernard, speaking of some, "we bear the detriment which Christ suffers with more equanimity than we should bear our own loss. We balance our daily expenses by a daily entrance of our gains, and we know nothing of the daily loss which happens to the flock of Christ."* It is not enough for a bishop to lead a holy life, and endeavour in his private conduct to imitate the virtues of Christ, unless he endeavours to make his subjects, or rather his children, holy, and tries to lead them, by making them follow in the footsteps of Christ, to eternal joy. Let those, then, who desire to suffer with Christ, to mourn with Him, and to compassionate Him in His sorrows, ever watch over His flock, never forsake His lambs, but direct them by their words, and lead them by their example.

Of the laity too might Christ reasonably complain, for neither sorrowing with Him, nor affording Him any relief in His sorrow. And if when hanging on the Cross He complained of the perfidy and obstinacy of the Jews, on whom His labours were lost, by whom His sorrows were ridiculed, and, as on so many madmen, the precious medicine of His Blood was wasted, how might He complain now at beholding, not from the Cross, but from heaven itself, those who believe in Him or profess to believe in Him, profit nothing by His Passion, tread His precious Blood under foot, and offer Him gall and vinegar by daily increasing their sins, without a thought of the divine judgment or a fear of the fire of hell.

* *De Consider.* lib. iv. cap. 9.

"*There shall be joy before the angels of God upon one sinner doing penance.*"* But is not this joy turned into sorrow, milk into gall, and wine into vinegar, when he who by faith and baptism has been born as it were in Christ, and who by the Sacrament of Penance has been resuscitated from death to life, within a short while after again kills his soul by a relapse into mortal sin? "*A woman when she is in labour hath sorrow, but when she hath brought forth the child, she remembereth no more the anguish, for joy that a man is born into the world.*"† But is not the mother afflicted with a twofold grief if the child dies immediately after death, or is still-born? So many work for their salvation by confessing their sins, perhaps even by fasting and alms-deeds, but their labour is in vain and they never obtain pardon for their sins, because they have a false conscience or are guilty of a culpable ignorance. Do not these labour, and labour uselessly, and afflict both themselves and their confessors with a double grief? Such people are like a sick man who accelerates his death by the use of a bitter medicine which he hoped would cure him; or like a gardener who bestows great pains on his vinery and grounds, and loses the whole fruit of his care by a sudden storm. These then are the evils we ought to deplore, and whosoever mourns and is afflicted thereat really grieves with Christ on the Cross, and whosoever labours according to his strength in lessening them, alleviates the sorrows and grief of his crucified Lord, and shall participate with Him in the joys of heaven, and shall reign for ever with Him in the kingdom of His heavenly Father.

* St. Luke xv. 10.   † St. John xvi. 21.

Chapter IX

The second fruit to be derived from the consideration of the fifth word spoken by Christ upon the Cross.

When I attentively meditate on the thirst which Christ endured on the Cross, another and very useful consideration occurs to me. Our Lord seems to me to have said, "*I thirst,*" in the same sense as that in which He addressed the Samaritan woman, "*Give Me to drink.*" For when He unfolded the mystery contained in these words, He added, "*If thou didst know the gift of God, and Who it is that saith to thee, Give Me to drink, thou perhaps wouldst have asked of Him, and He would have given thee living water.*"* Now, how could He thirst Who is the fount of living water? Does He not refer to Himself in saying, "*If any man thirst, let him come to Me and drink*"?† And is He not that rock of which the Apostle speaks: "*And they drank of the spiritual rock that followed them, and the rock was Christ*"?‡ In fine, is it not He Who addresses the Jews by the mouth of Jeremias the Prophet: "*They have forsaken Me the fountain of living water, and have digged to themselves cisterns, broken cisterns, that can hold no water*"?§ It seems to me, then, that our Lord from the Cross, as from a high throne, casts a look over the whole world, which is full of men who are athirst and fainting from exhaustion, and by reason of His parching state He pities the drought which mankind endures, and cries aloud "*I thirst,*" that is, I am thirsty on account of the dried and arid state of My body, but this thirst will quickly end. The thirst, however, that I suffer from My desire that men should begin by faith to know that I am the true fount of

---

* St. John iv. 7—10.   † St. John vii. 37.   ‡ 1 Cor. x. 4.
§ Jeremias ii. 13.

living water, should come to Me and drink, that they may not thirst for ever, is incomparably greater.

Oh, how happy should we be if we would but listen with attention to this address of the Word Incarnate! Does not every man almost thirst, with the burning and insatiable thirst of concupiscence, after the fleeting and turbid waters of transitory and perishable things, which are called goods, such as money, honour, pleasures? And who is there that has listened to the words of his Master, Christ, and has tasted the living water of heavenly wisdom, that has not felt a loathing for earthly things, and begun to aspire after those of heaven, who has not laid aside the morbid desire of acquiring and accumulating the things of this world and begun to aspire and long after those of heaven? This living water does not spring out of the earth, but comes down from heaven, and our Lord, Who is the fount of living water, will give it to us if we ask Him for it with fervent prayers and copious tears. Not only will it take away all eager longing for the things of earth, but will become an unfailing source of food and drink for us in this our exile. In this strain does Isaias speak: "*All you that thirst, come to the waters,*"* and that we may not think this water is precious or dear, he adds: "*Make haste, buy and eat; come ye, buy wine and milk without any price.*" It is called a water that must be bought, because it cannot be acquired without some effort, and without being in the proper dispositions for receiving it, but it is bought without silver or any bartering, because it is freely given, as it is invaluable. What the Prophet in one line calls water, he calls in the next wine and milk, because it is so efficacious as to embrace the qualities of water, wine, and milk.

True wisdom and charity is called water, because it cools the heat of concupiscence; it is called wine because

* Isaias lv. 1.

it warms and inebriates the mind with a sober ardour; it is called milk because it nourishes the young in Christ with a strengthening food, as St. Peter says: "*As new-born babes desire the rational milk.*"* This same true wisdom and charity—the very opposite to the concupiscence of the flesh—is that yoke which is sweet, that burden which is light, which those who take up willingly and humbly find to be a true and real rest to their souls, so that they no longer thirst, nor do they labour to draw water from earthly sources. This most enjoyable rest for the soul has filled deserts, peopled monasteries, reformed the clergy, restrained the married. The palace of Theodosius the Younger was not unlike a monastery; the house of Count Elizearius differed but little from a house of poor religious. Instead of oaths and quarrels, the Psalms and the sound of sacred music were heard there. All these blessings we owe to Christ, Who satiated our thirst at the price of His own suffering, and so watered the arid hearts of men that they will never more thirst, unless at the instigation of their enemy they wilfully withdraw themselves from that everlasting spring.

CHAPTER X.

The third fruit to be drawn from the consideration of the fifth word spoken by Christ upon the Cross.

The imitation of the patience of Christ is the third fruit to be gathered from the consideration of the fifth word. In the fourth word the humility of Christ, coupled with His patience, was conspicuous. In the fifth word His patience alone shines forth. Now, patience is not only one of the greatest virtues, but is positively the most

* 1 St. Peter ii. 2.

necessary for us. St. Cyprian says, "Amongst all the paths of heavenly training, I know of none more profitable for this life or advantageous for the next, than that those who strive in fear and devotion to obey the commandments of GOD, should above all things practise the virtue of patience." But before we speak of the necessity of patience we must distinguish the virtue from its counterfeit. True patience enables us to bear the misfortune of suffering without incurring the misfortune of sin. Such was the patience of the martyrs, who preferred to endure the tortures of the executioner rather than deny the faith of Christ, who preferred to suffer the loss of their earthly goods rather than worship false gods. The counterfeit of this virtue urges us to undergo every hardship to obey the law of concupiscence, to risk the loss of eternal happiness for the sake of a momentary pleasure. Such is the patience of the slaves of the devil who put up with hunger and thirst, cold and heat, loss of reputation, even of heaven itself, in order to increase their riches, to enjoy the pleasures of the flesh, or to gain a post of honour.

True patience has the property of increasing and preserving all other virtues. St. James is our authority for this eulogium of patience. He says, "*And patience hath a perfect work: that you may be perfect and entire, failing in nothing.*"* On account of the difficulties we meet with in the practise of virtue, none can flourish without patience, but when other virtues are accompanied by this one, all difficulties vanish, for patience renders crooked paths straight, and rough paths smooth. And this is so true that St. Cyprian, speaking of charity, the queen of virtues, cries out, "Charity, the bond of fraternity, the foundation of peace, the power and strength of union, is greater than faith or hope. It is the virtue from which martyrs derived their constancy, and it is the one we shall practise for ever

* St. James i. 4.

in the kingdom of heaven. But separate it from patience, and it will droop; take away from it the power of suffering and enduring, and it will wither and die."* The same Saint shows the necessity of this virtue also for preserving our chastity, uprightness, and peace with our neighbour. "If the virtue of patience is strongly and firmly rooted in your hearts, your body, which is holy and the temple of the living GOD, will not be polluted with adultery, your uprightness will not be sullied with the stain of injustice, nor after having fed on the Body of Christ will your hand be imbrued with blood." If we take these words in another way they show that without patience neither a chaste man will be able to preserve his purity, nor a just man be equitable, nor one who has received the Holy Eucharist be free from the evil effects of anger.

What St. James writes of the virtue of patience is taught in other words by the Prophet David, by our Lord, and his Apostle. In the ninth Psalm, David says, "*The patience of the poor shall not perish for ever*,"† because it has a perfect work, and consequently its fruit will never decay. Just as we are wont to say that the labours of the husbandman are profitable when they produce a good crop, and are useless when they bring forth nothing, so patience is said never to perish because its effects and rewards will remain for ever. In the text we have just quoted, the word *poor* is interpreted as meaning the humble man who confesses that he is poor and can neither do nor suffer anything without the help of GOD. In his treatise on patience,‡ St. Austin shows that not only the poor, but even the rich, may possess true patience, provided they trust not in themselves but in GOD, from Whom, as really in want of all divine gifts, they may ask and receive this favour. Our Lord seems to imply the same when He says in the Gospel, "*In your patience you shall possess your*

* Serm. *De Patientia*. † Psalm ix. 19. ‡ Cap. xv.

souls."* For they only really possess their souls, that is, their life as their own, and of which nothing can deprive them, who endure with patience every affliction, even death itself, in order not to sin against GOD. And although by death they appear to lose their souls, still they do not lose them, but preserve them for ever. For the death of the just is not death, but a sleep, and may even be regarded as a sleep of short duration. But the impatient, who in order to preserve the life of the body, do not hesitate to sin by denying Christ, by worshipping idols, by yielding to their lustful desires, or by committing some other crime, appear indeed to preserve their life for a time, but in reality lose the life both of body and soul for ever. And as of the really patient it may with truth be said, "*A hair of your head shall not perish,*"† so of the impatient might we with equal truth exclaim: There is not a single member of your body that will not be burnt in the fire of hell.

Lastly, the Apostle confirms our opinion: "*For patience is necessary for you, that doing the will of God you may receive the promise.*"‡ In this text St. Paul explicitly asserts patience to be not only useful, but even necessary in order to accomplish the will of GOD, and by accomplishing it to feel in ourselves the effect of His promise: "*To receive the crown of glory which God hath promised to them that love Him,*"§ and keep His commandments, for "*If any one love Me he will keep My word,*" and "*He that loveth Me not, keepeth not My words.*"|| So we see that the whole of Scripture teaches the faithful the necessity of the virtue of patience. For this reason Christ wished in the last moments of His life to declare that inward, and most bitter, and long endured suffering of His—His thirst —to encourage us by such an example to preserve our

---
* St. Luke xxi. 19.   † St. Luke xxi. 18.   ‡ Heb. x. 36.
§ St. James i. 12. || St. John xiv. 23, 24.

patience in every misfortune. That the thirst of Christ was a most vehement torture we have shown in the preceding chapter, that it was a long endured suffering we can easily prove.

To begin with the scourging at the pillar. When that took place Christ was already fatigued by His prolonged prayer and agony and sweat of blood in the Garden, by His many journeys to and fro during the night and the succeeding morning, from the Garden to the house of Annas, from the house of Annas to that of Caiphas, from the house of Caiphas to that of Pilate, from the house of Pilate to that of Herod, and from the house of Herod back again to Pilate. Moreover, from the time of the Last Supper our Lord had not tasted food or drink, or enjoyed a moment's repose, but had endured many and grievous insults in the house of Caiphas, was then cruelly scourged, which of itself was sufficient to produce a terrible thirst, and when the scourging was over His thirst, far from being satiated, was increased, for there followed the crowning with thorns and the mocking Him in derision. And when He had been crowned, His thirst, far from being satiated, was increased, for there followed the carrying of the Cross; and loaded with the instrument of His death, our wearied and exhausted Lord struggled up the hill of Calvary. When He arrived there they offered Him wine mixed with gall, which He tasted but would not drink. And so this journey was over at last, but the thirst that throughout the whole way had tortured our dear Lord, was undoubtedly increased. Then followed the crucifixion, and as the Blood flowed from His four wounds as from four fountains, every one may conceive how enormous His thirst must have been. Finally, for three successive hours, in the midst of a fearful darkness, we must again try to imagine with what a burning thirst that sacred Body was con-·ed. And although those that stood by offered vinegar to His mouth, still, as it was not wine or water, but a sharp and bitter draught, and that a very small draught, as He had to suck it up in drops from a sponge, we may without hesitation assert that our Redeemer from the very commencement of His Passion even to His death, endured with the most heroic patience this awful agony. Few of us can know by experience how great this suffering is, as we can find water anywhere to slake our thirst, but those who journey many days together in a desert sometimes learn what the torture of thirst is like.

Curtius relates that Alexander the Great was once marching through a desert with his army, and that after suffering all the deprivations of the want of water, they came up to a river, and the soldiers began to drink its waters with such eagerness, that many died in the very act, and he adds that "the number of those who perished on that occasion was greater than he had lost in any battle." Their burning thirst was so insupportable that the soldiers could not restrain themselves so far as to take breath whilst they were drinking, and consequently Alexander lost a great part of his army. There have been others who have suffered so much from thirst as to think muddy water, oil, blood, and other impure things, which no one would touch unless reduced by dire necessity, delicious. From this we may learn how great was the Passion of Christ, and how brilliantly His patience was displayed throughout. GOD grant that we may know this, imitate it, and by suffering together with Christ here, come to reign with Him hereafter.

But I fancy that I hear some pious souls exclaim that they are eager and anxious to know by what means they can best imitate the patience of Christ, and be able to say with the Apostle, "*With Christ I am nailed to the Cross*,"* and with St. Ignatius the Martyr, "My Love is crucified."†

* Gal. ii. 19.   † *Epist. ad Rom.*

It is not so difficult as many imagine. It is not necessary for all to lie on the ground, to scourge themselves to blood, to fast daily on bread and water, to wear a coarse haircloth, an iron chain, or other instruments of penance for conquering the flesh, and crucifying it with its vices and concupiscences. These practices are praiseworthy and useful, provided they are not injurious to one's health, or performed without the sanction of one's director. But I desire to show my pious readers a means of practising the virtue of patience, and of imitating our meek and gentle Redeemer, which all may embrace, which contains nothing extraordinary, nothing new, and from the use of which no one can be suspected of seeking to gain applause for his sanctity.

In the first place, then, he who loves the virtue of patience ought cheerfully to submit to those labours and sorrows with which we are assured by faith it is the Divine will we should be afflicted, according to those words of the Apostle: *"For patience is necessary for you: that doing the will of God, you may receive the promise."** Now, what GOD wishes us to embrace is neither difficult for me to show or for my readers to learn. All the commandments of our holy mother the Church must be kept with loving obedience and patience, no matter how hard or difficult they may appear. What are these commandments of the Church? The fasts of Lent, of the Ember days, and of certain vigils. To keep these religiously as they ought to be kept, will require a great amount of patience. Now, suppose a person on a fast-day sits down to a well spread dinner-table, or in the single meal that he is allowed eats as much as he would at any two meals on an ordinary day, or anticipates the time for his collation, or eats more than he is allowed, such a person will certainly neither hunger nor thirst, nor will his patience produce fruit. But if he

* Heb. x. 36.

firmly resolves not to take food before the appointed time, unless sickness or some other necessity obliges him, and to take food that is coarse and common and suitable to a time of penance, and does not exceed what he usually takes at a single meal, but gives to the poor all that he would eat if it were not a fast day, as St. Leo advises: "Let the poor be fed by what those that fast abstain from;" and elsewhere, "Let us feel hunger for a little time, dearly beloved, and for a short while let us diminish what we want for our own comfort, in order to be of service to the poor;" and if at eventide he allows the collation to be nothing more than a collation; in such a case undoubtedly patience will be necessary to bear our hunger and thirst, and thus by fasting we shall imitate as far as we are able the patience of Christ, and shall be nailed in part at least to the Cross with Him. But some one may object, all these things are not absolutely necessary. I grant it; but they are necessary if we desire to practise the virtue of patience, or become like our suffering Redeemer. Again, our holy mother the Church orders ecclesiastics and religious to recite or sing the canonical hours. Now, we shall require all the assistance which the virtue of patience can give us, if this sacred reading and prayer is to be performed in the manner in which it ought to be, as there are few who have not enough to do to keep themselves free from distractions during prayer. Many hurry through their prayers as quickly as possible, as though they were undertaking a very laborious duty, and wished to free themselves from the burden in the shortest possible time, and then they say their office, not standing up or kneeling down, but sitting or walking about, just as if the fatigue of prayer would be lessened by sitting or lightened by walking. I am speaking of those who say their Office in private, not of those who sing it in choir. Again, in order not to break into their sleep, many recite during the day that part of the Office which the Church has ordered to be said during the night. I say nothing of the attention and the elevation of mind that is required whilst GOD is invoked in prayer, because many think of what they sing or read less than of anything else. Indeed it is surprising that many more do not see how necessary the virtue of patience is to take away the repugnance we feel to spend a long time in prayer, to rise so as to say the canonical hours at the proper time, to bear the fatigue of standing or of kneeling, to prevent our thoughts from wandering, and to keep them fixed on the one thing we are engaged in. Let my readers listen to an account of the devotion with which St. Francis of Assisi recited his Breviary, and they will then learn that the Divine Office cannot be said without the exercise of the greatest patience. In his Life of St. Francis, St. Bonaventure speaks thus: "This holy man was wont to recite the Divine Office with no less fear than devotion towards GOD, and although he suffered great pains in his eyes, stomach, spleen, and liver, he would neither lean against any wall or partition whilst he sang, but standing erect, without his hood, he kept his eyes fixed, and had the appearance of a person in a swoon. If he was on a journey he would keep to his regular time, and recite the Divine Office in the usual manner, no matter if a violent rain was falling. He thought himself guilty of a serious fault if during its recital he allowed his mind to be occupied with vain thoughts, and as often as this happened he hastened to confession to make atonement for it. He recited the Psalms with such attention of mind as if he had GOD present before him, and whenever the name of the Lord occurred he would smack his lips from the sweetness which the pronunciation of that name had left behind it." As soon as any one endeavours to recite the Divine Office in this manner, and to rise at night to recite his Matins, Lauds, and Prime, he will learn by

·experience that labour and patience are necessary for the due performance of this duty. There are many other things which the Church, guided by the Holy Scriptures, lays down for us as the will of GOD, and for the due fulfilment of these also we require the virtue of patience; such as to give to the poor from our superfluity, to pardon those that injure us, to make satisfaction to those whom we have injured, to confess our sins at least once a year, and to receive the Blessed Eucharist, which requires no small preparation. All this demands patience, but by way of example I will explain a few more things at greater length.

Everything which either devils or men do to afflict us is another indication of the Divine will, and another call for the exercise of our patience. When bad men and evil spirits try us, their object is to injure not to benefit us. Still GOD, without Whom they can do nothing, would not allow any storm to break upon us, unless He judged it to be useful, consequently every affliction may be regarded as coming from the hand of GOD, and should therefore be borne with patience and cheerfulness. Holy and upright Job knew that the misfortunes with which he was stricken, and which deprived him in one day of all his riches, of all his sons, and then of his bodily health, proceeded from the hatred of the devil, yet he exclaimed: "*The Lord gave, and the Lord hath taken away, blessed be the name of the Lord,*"* because he knew that his calamities could only happen by the will of GOD. I do not say this because I think that when any one is persecuted either by his fellow-creatures or by the devil, he should not, or ought not to do his best to recover his losses, to consult a physician if unwell, or to defend himself and his property, but I merely give this advice, not to bear any revenge against evil men, not to return evil for evil, but to bear misfortune with

* Job i. 21.

patience because our GOD wishes us to do so, and by fulfilling His will we shall receive the promise.

The last thing I wish to observe is this. We must all strive to be intimately convinced that everything which happens by chance or accident, as a great drought, too much rain, pestilence, famine, and the like, do not happen without the special providence and will of GOD, and consequently we should not complain of the elements, or of GOD Himself, but should regard evils of this kind as a scourge with which GOD punishes us for our sins, and bowing ourselves beneath His almighty hand, bear everything in humility and patience. GOD will thus be appeased. He will scatter his benedictions upon us. He will chastise us as His sons with a fatherly love, and will not deprive us of the kingdom of heaven. We may learn what is the reward of patience from an example which St. Gregory adduces. In the thirty-fifth homily on the Gospels, he says that a certain man Stephen was so patient as to consider those that oppressed him his greatest friends; he returned thanks for insults; he looked upon misfortunes as gains; he counted his enemies in the number of his well-wishers and benefactors. The world considered him as a fool and madman, but he turned no deaf ear to the words of the Apostle of Christ: "*If any man among you seem to be wise in this world, let him become a fool that he may be wise*,"* and St. Gregory adds that when he was dying many angels were seen assisting round his couch, who carried his soul straight to heaven, and the holy Doctor did not hesitate to rank Stephen amongst the martyrs on account of his extraordinary patience.

* 1 Cor. iii. 18.

CHAPTER XI.

The fourth fruit to be drawn from the consideration of the fifth word spoken by Christ upon the Cross.

There remains one fruit more, and that the sweetest of all, to be gathered from the consideration of this word. St. Austin, in his explanation of the word "*I thirst,*" which is to be found in his treatise on the sixty-eighth Psalm, says that it shows not only the desire which Christ had for drink, but still more the desire with which He was inflamed that His enemies should believe in Him and be saved. We may advance a step further than St. Austin, and say that Christ thirsted for the glory of GOD and the salvation of men, and we ought to thirst for the glory of GOD, for the honour of Christ, for our own salvation, and the salvation of our brethren. We cannot doubt that Christ thirsted for the glory of His Father, and the salvation of souls, for all His works, all His preaching, all His sufferings, all His miracles proclaimed it. We must consider what we have to do not to show ourselves ungrateful to such a Benefactor, and what means we must take to become so inflamed as really to thirst for the glory of that GOD Who "*so loved the world as to give His only-begotten Son;*"* and fervently and ardently thirst for the honour of Christ, Who "*loved us, and delivered Himself for us an oblation and a sacrifice to God for an odour of sweetness,*"† and so feelingly compassionate our brethren as zealously to desire their salvation. Still the most necessary thing for ourselves is so cordially and earnestly to long for our own salvation, that this desire should compel us, according to our strength, to think and speak and do everything that can help us to save our souls. If we care nothing for the

* St. John iii. 16. † Ephes. v. 2.

honour of GOD, or the glory of Christ, and feel no anxiety for our own salvation or that of others, it follows that GOD will be deprived of the honour which is His due, that Christ will lose the glory which is His own, that our neighbour will not reach heaven, and that we ourselves shall perish miserably for eternity. And on this account I am often filled with astonishment when I reflect that we all know how sincerely Christ thirsted for our salvation, and we, who believe Christ to be the Wisdom of the living GOD, are not moved to imitate His example in a matter so intimately connected with ourselves. Nor am I less astonished to see men hunt after worldly goods with such avidity, as though there were no heaven, and so little trouble themselves about their salvation, that far from thirsting for it, they scarcely give it a passing thought, as though it were a trivial matter of light importance. Moreover temporal goods, which are not unmixed pleasures, but are accompanied with many misfortunes, are sought after with earnestness and anxiety; but eternal happiness, which is an unalloyed pleasure, is cared for so little, longed for so unconcernedly, as though it possessed no advantage whatever. Enlighten, O Lord, the eyes of my soul, that I may find the cause of such a hurtful indifference.

Love produces desire, and desire, when it is excessive, is called a thirst. Now who is there that cannot love His own eternal happiness, particularly when that happiness is free from everything that can mar it? And if so great a prize cannot but be loved, why cannot it be ardently desired, eagerly sought after, and with all our strength thirsted for? Perhaps the reason is that our salvation is not a matter that falls under the senses, we have never had any experience of what it is like, as we have had in matters that regard the body, and so we are solicitous for the latter, and coldly indifferent to the former. But if such is the case, why did David, who was a mortal man like ourselves, so eagerly long for the vision of GOD, and the happiness of heaven consists in the vision of GOD, as to cry out: "*As the hart panteth after the fountains of water, so my soul panteth after Thee, O God. My soul hath thirsted after the strong living God; when shall I come and appear before the face of God?*"* David is not the only one in this vale of tears who has desired with such a burning desire the sight of the vision of GOD; there have been several others also, who were distinguished by their holiness, by whom the things of this world were regarded as mean and insipid, and to whom the thought and the remembrance of GOD was alone agreeable and most charming. The reason then why we do not thirst for our eternal happiness is not because heaven is invisible, but because we do not think of what is before us with attention, with assiduity, with faith. And the reason why we do not regard heavenly things as we ought is that we are not spiritual, but sensual men: "*The sensual man perceiveth not those things that are of the spirit of God.*"† Wherefore, my soul, if you desire for your own salvation, and that of your neighbour, if you have at heart the honour of GOD and the glory of Christ, listen to the words of the blessed Apostle St. James: "*If any of you want wisdom, let Him ask of God, Who giveth to all men abundantly, and upbraideth not, and it shall be given him.*"‡ This sublime wisdom is not to be acquired in the schools of this world, but in the school of the Holy Spirit of GOD, Who changes the sensual man into the spiritual one. But it is not enough to ask for this wisdom once only and with coldness, but to demand it with much groaning from our heavenly Father. For if a father according to the flesh cannot refuse his son when he asks for bread, "*how much more will your Father from heaven give the Good Spirit to them that ask Him.*"§

* Psalm xli. 2, 3.   † 1 Cor. ii. 14.   ‡ St. James i. 5.   § St. Luke xi. 13.

CHAPTER XII.

The literal explanation of the sixth word, "It is consummated."

The sixth word spoken by our Lord on the Cross is mentioned by St. John as being in a manner joined with the fifth word. For as soon as our Lord had said, "*I thirst,*" and had tasted the vinegar which was offered Him, St. John adds: "*Jesus therefore when He had tasted the vinegar, said: It is consummated.*"* And indeed nothing can be added to the simple words, "*It is consummated,*" except that the work of the Passion was now perfected and completed. GOD the Father had imposed two duties on His Son: the first to preach the Gospel; the other to suffer for mankind. Of the first Christ had already said, "*I have glorified Thee on earth: I have finished the work which Thou gavest Me to do.*"† Our Lord spoke these words after he had concluded the long and farewell address to His disciples at the Last Supper. Then He had accomplished the first work which His Heavenly Father had imposed upon Him. The second task, of drinking the bitter cup of His chalice, remained. He had alluded to this when He asked the two sons of Zebedee, "*Can you drink the chalice that I shall drink?*"‡ and again, "*Father, if Thou wilt, remove this chalice from Me;*"§ and elsewhere, "*The chalice which My Father hath given Me, shall I not drink it?*"|| Of this task, Christ at the point of death could now exclaim, "*It is consummated,* for I have drained the chalice of suffering to the dregs: nothing now remains

---

* St. John xix. 30. † St. John xvii. 4.
‡ St. Matt. xx. 22. § St. Luke xxii. 42. || St. John xviii. 11.

for Me but to die. *And bowing His head, He gave up the ghost.*"*

But as neither our Lord nor St. John, who were both concise in what they said, have explained what was consummated, we have the opportunity of applying the word with great reason and advantage to several mysteries. St. Augustine, in his commentary on this passage, refers the word to the fulfilment of all the prophecies that had reference to our Lord. "*Afterwards Jesus knowing that all things were now accomplished, that the Scripture might be fulfilled, said, I thirst,*" and, "*when He had taken the vinegar, said, It is consummated,*"† which means that what remained to be accomplished has been accomplished, and so we may conclude that our Lord wished to show that everything which had been foretold by the prophets concerning His life and death had been brought to pass and fulfilled. Indeed, all the predictions had been verified. His conception: "*Behold, a Virgin shall conceive, and bear a Son.*"‡ His nativity at Bethlehem: "*And thou, Bethlehem Ephrata, art a little one among the thousands of Juda; out of thee shall He come forth unto Me that is to be the ruler in Israel.*"§ The apparition of a new star: "*A star shall rise out of Jacob.*"‖ The adoration of the Kings: "*The Kings of Tharsis and the islands shall offer presents, the Kings of the Arabians and of Saba shall bring gifts.*"¶ The preaching of the Gospel: "*The Spirit of the Lord is upon Me, because the Lord hath anointed Me: He hath sent Me to preach to the meek, to heal the contrite of heart, and to preach a release to the captives, and deliverance to them that are shut up.*"** His miracles: "*God Himself will come and will save you. Then shall the eyes of the blind be opened,*

---

* St. John xix. 30. † St. John xix. 28, 30.
‡ Isaias vii. 14. § Micheas v. 2. ‖ Numbers xxiv. 17.
¶ Psalm lxxi. 10. ** Isaias lxi. 1.

and the ears of the deaf shall be unstopped. Then shall the lame man leap as a hart, and the tongue of the dumb shall be free."* His sitting upon the ass: "*Behold thy King will come to thee, the Just and Saviour: He is poor and riding upon an ass, and upon a colt the foal of an ass.*"† And the whole Passion had been graphically foretold by David in the Psalms, by Isaias, Jeremias, Zacharias, and others. This is the meaning of what our Lord said when He was about to set out for His Passion: "*Behold we go up to Jerusalem, and all things shall be accomplished which were written by the prophets concerning the Son of Man.*"‡ Of those things therefore which had to be accomplished, He now says, "*It is consummated;*" everything is finished, so that what the prophets foretold is now found to be true.

In the second place, St. John Chrysostom says that the word, "*It is consummated,*" shows that the power which had been given to men and devils over the person of Christ has been taken away from them by the death of Christ. When our Lord said to the Chief Priests and masters of the Temple, "*This is your hour and the power of darkness,*"§ He alluded to this power. The whole period of time, then, during which, by the permission of GOD, the wicked had power over Christ, was brought to a close when He exclaimed, "*It is consummated,*" for then the peregrination of the Son of GOD amongst men, which Baruch had foretold, came to an end: "*This is our God, and there shall no other be accounted of in comparison of Him. He found out all the way of knowledge, and gave it to Jacob His servant, and to Israel His beloved. Afterwards He was seen upon earth, and conversed with men.*"‖ And together with His pilgrimage that condition of

---

* Isaias xxxv. 4, 5, 6.   † Zach. ix. 9.   ‡ St. Luke xviii. 31.
§ St. Luke xxii. 53.   ‖ Baruch iii. 36—38.

His mortal life was ended, according to which He hungered and thirsted, He slept and was fatigued, was subject to affronts and scourgings, to wounds and to death. And so when Christ on the Cross exclaimed, "*It is consummated, and bowing His head He gave up the ghost,*" He ended the journey of which He had said, "*I came forth from the Father, and am come into the world, again I leave the world and I go to the Father.*"* That laborious pilgrimage was ended of which Jeremias had said, "*O expectation of Israel, the Saviour thereof in time of trouble: why wilt Thou be as a stranger in the land, and as a wayfaring man turning in to lodge.*"† The subjection of His Human Nature to death was ended, the power of His enemies over Himself was ended.

In the third place was ended the greatest of all sacrifices, in comparison to which real and true sacrifice all the sacrifices of the Old Law were regarded as mere shadows and figures. St. Leo says, "Thou hast drawn all things to Thyself, O Lord, for when the veil of the Temple was rent, the Holy of Holies departed from unworthy priests: figures became truths: prophecies became manifest: the Law became the Gospel." And a little later, "By the cessation of a variety of sacrifices in which victims were offered, the one oblation of Thy Body and Blood makes up for the differences of the victims."‡ For in this one Sacrifice of Christ, the priest is the GOD-Man, the altar is the Cross, the victim is the Lamb of GOD, the fire for the holocaust is charity, the fruit of the sacrifice is the redemption of the world. The priest, I say, was the GOD-Man, than Whom no one is greater: "*Thou art a priest for ever according to the order of Melchisedech;*"§ and rightly according to the order of Melchisedech, because

---

* St. John xvi. 28.   † Jer. xiv. 8.   ‡ Serm. 8. De Pass. Dom.
§ Psalm cix. 4.

we read in Scripture that Melchisedech was without father or mother or genealogy, and Christ was without a father on earth, without a mother in heaven, and without genealogy, for "*who shall declare His generation;*"* "*from the womb before the day-star I begot Thee;*"† "*and His going forth is from the beginning, from the days of eternity.*"‡ The altar was the Cross. And as previous to the time when Christ suffered upon it, it was the sign of the greatest ignominy, so now has it become dignified and ennobled, and on the last day shall appear in the heaven more brilliant than the sun. The Church applies to the Cross the words of the Evangelist: "*Then shall appear the sign of the Son of Man in heaven,*"§ for she sings: "This sign of the Cross shall appear in heaven when the Lord shall come to judge." St. John Chrysostom confirms this opinion, and observes that when "*the sun shall be darkened, and the moon shall not give her light,*"‖ the Cross shall be seen more brilliant than the sun in its mid-day splendour. The victim was the Lamb of GOD, all innocent and immaculate, of whom Isaias said, "*He shall be led as a sheep to the slaughter, and shall be dumb as a lamb before His shearer, and He shall not open His mouth,*"¶ and of Whom His Precursor exclaimed, "*Behold the Lamb of God, behold Him Who taketh away the sin of the world,*"** and St. Peter: "*Knowing that you were not redeemed with corruptible things as gold or silver, but with the precious Blood of Christ, as of a lamb unspotted and undefiled.*"†† He is called also in the Apocalypse, "*The Lamb which was slain from the beginning of the world,*"‡‡ because the merit of His Sacrifice was foreseen by GOD, and was of advantage to those who lived

---

* Isaias liii. 8.   † Psalm cix. 3.   ‡ Micheas v. 2.
§ St. Matt. xxiv. 30.   ‖ St. Matt. xxiv. 29.   ¶ Isaias liii. 7.
** St. John i. 29.   †† 1 St. Peter i. 18, 19.   ‡‡ Apoc. xiii. 8.

before the coming of Christ. The fire which consumes the holocaust, and completes the Sacrifice, is the immense love which, as in a heated furnace, burnt in the Heart of the Son of GOD, and which the many waters of His Passion could not extinguish. Lastly, the fruit of the Sacrifice was the atonement for the sins of all the children of Adam, or in other words, the reconciliation of the whole world with GOD. St. John in his first Epistle says, "*He is the propitiation for our sins: and not for ours only, but also for those of the whole world*,"* and this is only another way of expressing the idea of St. John Baptist: "*Behold the Lamb of God, behold Him Who taketh away the sin of the world.*"† One difficulty here arises. How could Christ be at one and the same time priest and victim, since it is the duty of the priest to slay the victim? Now, Christ did not slay Himself, nor could He do so, for if He had He would have committed a sacrilege and not have offered a sacrifice. It is true Christ did not slay Himself, still He offered a real sacrifice, because He willingly and cheerfully offered Himself to death for the glory of GOD and the salvation of men. For neither could the soldiers have apprehended Him, nor the nails have transfixed His hands and feet, nor death, although He was fastened to the Cross, have had any power over Him unless He Himself had wished it. Consequently, with great truth did Isaias say, "*He was offered, because it was His own will;*"‡ and our Lord: "*I lay down My life; no man taketh it away from Me, but I lay it down of Myself;*"§ and more clearly still St. Paul: "*Christ also hath loved us, and hath delivered Himself for us, an oblation and a sacrifice to God for an odour of sweetness.*"‖ In a wonderful manner therefore was it arranged that all the evil, all the sin, all the crime committed in putting Christ to death was committed by Judas

* 1 St. John ii. 2. † St. John i. 29.
‡ Isaias liii. 7.   § St. John x. 17, 18.   ‖ Ephes. v. 2.

and the Jews, by Pilate and the soldiers. These offered no sacrifice, but were guilty of sacrilege, and deserve to be called, not priests, but sacrilegious wretches. And all the virtue, all the holiness, all the dutifulness displayed in the Passion, were the virtue and the holiness and the dutifulness of Christ, Who offered Himself a victim to GOD by patiently enduring death, even the death of the Cross, in order to appease the anger of His Father, to reconcile mankind to GOD, to make satisfaction to the Divine justice, and to save the fallen race of Adam. St. Leo beautifully expresses this thought in a few words: "He allowed the impure hands of wretches to be turned against Himself, and they became cooperators with the Redeemer at the time they were committing a heinous sin."

In the fourth place, by the death of Christ the mighty struggle between Himself and the prince of the world was brought to a close. In alluding to this struggle, our Lord made use of these words: "*Now this is the judgment of the world. Now shall the prince of this world be cast out. And I, if I be lifted up from the earth, will draw all things to Myself.*"* This struggle was a judicial, not a military one; it was a struggle between rival suitors, not between rival armies. Satan disputed with Christ the possession of the world, the dominion over mankind. For a long time the devil had unlawfully thrust himself into possession, because he had overcome the first man, and had made him and all his descendants his slaves. For this reason St. Paul calls the devils, "*the principalities and powers, the rulers of the world of this darkness.*"† And as we said a little before, even Christ calls the devil "*the prince of this world.*" Now the devil did not wish merely to be the prince, but even the god of this world, and so the Psalmist exclaims: "*For all the gods of the Gentiles are*

---

* St. John xii. 31, 32.   † Ephes. vi. 12.

devils, but the Lord made the heavens."* Satan was adored in the idols of the Gentiles, and was worshipped in their sacrifices of lambs and calves. On the other side, the Son of GOD, as the true and lawful heir of the universe, demanded the principality of this world for Himself. This was the contest which was decided on the Cross, and judgment was pronounced in favour of our Lord JESUS CHRIST, because on the Cross He fully atoned for the sins of the first man and of all his children. For the obedience shown to the Eternal Father by His Son was greater than the disobedience of a servant to his master, and the humility with which the Son of GOD died on the Cross redounded more to the honour of the Father than the pride of a servant tended to His injury. So GOD by the merits of His Son was reconciled to mankind, and mankind was snatched from the power of the devil, and *"translated into the kingdom of the Son of His love."*†

There is another reason which St. Leo adduces, and we will give it in his own words. "If our proud and cruel enemy could have known the plan which the mercy of GOD had adopted, he would have restrained the passions of the Jews, and not have goaded them on by unjust hatred, in order that he might not lose his power over all his captives by fruitlessly attacking the liberty of One Who owed him nothing." This is an exceedingly weighty reason. For it is just that the devil should lose his authority over all those who by sin had become his slaves, because he had dared to lay his hands on Christ, Who was not his slave, Who had never sinned, and Whom he nevertheless persecuted even unto death. Now, if such is the state of the case, if the battle is over, if the Son of GOD has gained the victory, and if *"He will have all men to be saved,"*‡ how is it that so many are in the power of the

* Psalm xcv. 5.   † Coloss. i. 13.   ‡ 1 Tim. ii. 4.

devil in this life, and suffer the torments of hell in the next? I answer in one word: They wish it. Christ came victorious out of the contest, after bestowing two unspeakable favours on the human race. The first of opening to the just the gates of heaven, which had been closed from the fall of Adam to that day, and on the day of His victory He said to the thief who had been justified by the merits of His Blood, through faith, hope, and charity: "*This day thou shalt be with Me in Paradise;*"* and the Church in her exultation cries out, "Thou having overcome the sting of death, hast opened to believers the kingdom of heaven." The second, of instituting the sacraments which have the power of remitting sin and of conferring grace. He sends the preachers of His Word to all parts of the world to proclaim: "*He that believeth, and is baptized, shall be saved.*"† And so our victorious Lord has opened a way to all to attain the glorious liberty of the sons of GOD, and if there are any who are unwilling to enter on this way, they perish by their own fault, and not by the want of power or the want of will of their Redeemer.

In the fifth place, the word, "*It is consummated,*" may rightly be applied to the completion of the building, that is, the Church. Christ our Master uses this very word in reference to a building: *Hic homo cœpit ædificare et non potuit consummare*—"*This man began to build and was not able to finish.*"‡ The Fathers teach that the foundation of the Church was laid when Christ was baptized, and the building completed when He died. Epiphanius in his third book against heretics, and St. Augustine in the last book of the City of GOD, show that Eve, who was built from a rib of Adam whilst he was asleep, typifies the Church, which was built from the side of Christ whilst He

---

* St. Luke xxiii. 43.
† St. Mark xvi. 16.   ‡ St. Luke xiv. 30.

slept in death. And they remark that not without reason does the author of the Book of Genesis use the word built, not formed. St. Augustine* proves that the building of the Church commenced with the baptism of Christ, from the words of the Psalmist: *"And He shall rule from sea to sea, and from the river unto the ends of the earth."*† The kingdom of Christ, which is the Church, began with the baptism He received at the hands of St. John, by which He consecrated the waters and instituted that sacrament which is the gate of the Church, and when the voice of His Father was clearly heard in the heavens: *"This is My beloved Son, in Whom I am well pleased."*‡ From that moment our Lord began to preach and to gather disciples, who were the first children of the Church. And all the sacraments derive their efficacy from the Passion of Christ, although our Lord's side was opened after His death, and blood and water, which typify the two chief sacraments of the Church, flowed forth. The flowing of blood and water from the side of Christ after death was a sign of the sacraments, not their institution. We may conclude then that the building of the Church was completed when Christ said, "*It is consummated,*" because nothing then remained but death, which immediately followed, and consummated the price of our redemption.

* *De Civit.* l. 27, c. 8.   † Psalm lxxi. 8.   ‡ St. Matt. iii. 17.

CHAPTER XIII.

The first fruit to be drawn from the consideration of the sixth word spoken by Christ upon the Cross.

Whoever attentively ponders on the sixth word must derive many advantages from his reflections. St. Augustine draws a most useful lesson from the fact that the word *"It is consummated"* shows the fulfilment of all prophecies that had reference to our Lord. For as we are certain from what has happened that the prophecies regarding our Lord were true, so ought we to be equally certain that other things which the same Prophets foretold, and which have not yet come to pass, are equally true. The Prophets spoke not of their own will, but were inspired by the Holy Ghost, and because the Holy Ghost is GOD, Who cannot either deceive or mislead, we should be most confident that everything which they foretold will come to pass, if it has not done so already. "For as heretofore," says St. Augustine, "everything has been accomplished, so what has to be fulfilled will assuredly happen. Let us then stand in awe of the day of judgment, for the Lord will come. He who came as a lowly Babe will come as a mighty GOD." We have more reasons than the saints of old for never wavering in our faith, or in our belief in what is to come. Those who lived before the coming of Christ were obliged to believe, without proof, many things for which we have abundant testimony, and from what has been fulfilled we may easily deduce that the remaining prophecies will be accomplished. The contemporaries of Noe heard of the universal Deluge, not only from the lips of the prophet of GOD, but from his conduct in working so diligently at the construction of the Ark; still they were hard to convince, as never before had there been a deluge, or anything similar to it, and consequently the Divine wrath overtook them unawares. As we know what Noe foretold came to pass, we should have no difficulty in believing that the world and everything we now esteem so much will one day be destroyed by fire. Still, there are very few who have such a lively faith in this as to detach themselves from perishable things, and fix their hearts on the joys above, which are real and everlasting.

The terrors of the last day have been foretold by Christ Himself, so that those are altogether inexcusable who cannot be induced to believe that because some prophecies have been fulfilled, therefore others will be. These are the words of Christ: "*And as in the days of Noe, so shall also the coming of the Son of Man be. For as in the days before the flood, they were eating and drinking, marrying, and giving in marriage, even till that day in which Noe entered into the ark. And they knew not till the Flood came and took them all away; so also shall the coming of the Son of Man be. Watch ye, therefore, because you know not at what hour your Lord will come.*"* And St. Peter says: "*The day of the Lord shall come as a thief, in which the heavens shall pass away with great violence, and the elements shall be melted with heat, and the earth, and the works which are in it shall be burnt up.*"† But some may argue, all these things are a long way off. Let it be that they are a long way off, and if they are, the day of death is certainly not far off: its hour is very uncertain, and yet it is certain that in the particular judgment which is close at hand, an account will have to be rendered of every idle word; and if of every idle word, what of sinful words, of blasphemies which are so common? and if an account of every word is to be ren-

* St. Matt. xxiv. 37, 38, 39, 42. † 2 St. Peter iii. 10.

dered, what of actions, of thefts, adulteries, frauds, murders, injustice, and other mortal sins? Therefore the fulfilment of some prophecies will render us all the more blameworthy if we do not believe that the other prophecies will be accomplished. Nor is it enough merely to believe, unless our faith efficaciously moves our will to do or to avoid what our understanding teaches us should be done or avoided. If an architect were to give it as his opinion that a house was about to fall, and the inhabitants were to acknowledge that they believed the architect's words, but still would not abandon the house, and were buried in its ruins, what would people say of such faith? They would say with the Apostle: "*They profess that they know God; but in their works they deny Him.*"* Or what would be said if a doctor were to order a patient not to drink wine, and the patient were to own that the advice was good, but were to continue to drink wine, and be angry if it was not given him? Should we not say that such a patient was mad and had no confidence in his physician? Would that there were not so many Christians who profess to believe in the judgments of God and other things, and by their conduct give a denial to their words.

Chapter XIV.

The second fruit to be drawn from the consideration of the sixth word spoken by Christ upon the Cross.

Another advantage may be derived from the second interpretation which we gave of the word "*It is consummated.*" With St. John Chrysostom, we said that by His death Christ finished his laborious sojourn amongst us.

* Titus i. 16.

No one can deny but that His mortal life was beyond measure bitter, but its very bitterness was compensated for by its shortness, by its fruit, by its glory, and by its honour. It lasted thirty-three years. What is a labour of thirty-three years compared to an eternity of rest? Our Lord laboured in hunger and thirst, in the midst of many griefs, of insults without number, of blows, of wounds, of death itself; but now He drinks from the fount of joys, and His joy shall last for ever. Again, He was humbled, and for a short time was "*the reproach of men and the outcast of the people;*"* but "*God hath exalted Him, and hath given Him a name which is above all names, that in the name of Jesus every knee should bow, of those that are in heaven, on earth, and under the earth.*"† On the other hand, the perfidious Jews for an hour exulted over Christ in His sufferings; Judas for an hour enjoyed the price of his avarice, a few pieces of silver; Pilate for an hour gloried because he had not lost the friendship of Augustus, and had regained that of Herod; but for nearly two thousand years they have all been suffering the torments of hell and their cries of despair will be heard for ever and for ever. From their misfortune all the servants of the cross may learn how good and profitable a thing it is to be humble, to be meek, to be patient, to carry their cross in this present life, to follow Christ as their guide, and by no means to envy those who appear to be happy in this world. The lives of Christ and of His Apostles and Martyrs are a true commentary on the words of the Master of masters. "*Blessed are the poor, blessed are the meek, blessed are they that mourn; blessed are they that suffer persecution for justice' sake, for theirs is the kingdom of heaven.*‡ And on the other hand, "*Wo to you who are rich, for you have your consolation. Wo to you that are filled, for you shall hunger. Wo to you that*

---

* Psalm xxi. 7. † Philipp. ii. 9, 10. ‡ St. Matt. v. 3, 10.

*now laugh, for you shall mourn and weep."** Although neither the words nor the life and death of Christ are understood or put in practice by the world, still, whoever wishes to leave the bustle of life and enter into his heart and seriously meditate and say to himself, "*I will hear what the Lord God will speak in me*,"† and importunes His Divine Master with humble prayer and groaning of spirit, will without difficulty understand all truth, and the truth shall free him from all errors, and what before appeared impossible will become easy.

CHAPTER XV.

The third fruit to be drawn from the consideration of the sixth word spoken by Christ upon the Cross.

The third fruit to be gathered from the consideration of the sixth word is, that we should learn to become spiritual priests, "*to offer up to God spiritual sacrifices*," ‡ as St. Peter tell us, or as St. Paul advises us, "*to present*" our "*bodies a living sacrifice, holy, pleasing unto God,*" our "*reasonable service.*"§ For if this word "*It is finished*" shows us that the sacrifice of our High Priest has been accomplished on the Cross, it is just and proper that the disciples of a crucified GOD, who are desirous, as far as they can, of imitating their Master, should offer themselves as a sacrifice to GOD according to their weakness and their poverty. Indeed, St. Peter says that all Christians are priests, not strictly so indeed as those are who are ordained by bishops in the Holy Roman Church for offering the sacrifice of the Body and Blood of Christ, but spiritual priests for offering spiritual victims, not such victims as

---

* St. Luke vi. 24, 25. † Psalm lxxxiv. 9.
‡ 1 St. Peter ii. 5. § Rom. xii. 1.

we read of in the Old Testament—sheep and oxen, turtles and doves—or the Victim of the New Testament—the Body of Christ in the Blessed Eucharist, but mystical victims which can be offered by all, as prayer and praise and good works and fasts and almsdeeds, as St. Paul says, "*Let us offer the sacrifice of praise always to God, that is to say, the fruit of lips confessing to His name.*"* In his Epistle to the Romans, the same Apostle most distinctly tells us to offer to GOD the mystical sacrifice of our bodies after the sacrifices of the Old Law, which were regulated by four decrees. The first was, that the victim should be something consecrated to GOD, which it would be unlawful to turn to any profane use. The second, that the victim should be a living creature, as a sheep, a goat, or a calf. The third, that it should be holy, that is, clean; for the Jews considered some animals clean, others unclean. Sheep, oxen, goats, turtles, sparrows, and doves were clean; whereas the horse, the lion, the fox, the hawk, the raven, and others were unclean. The fourth, that the victim should be burnt, and should send forth an odour of sweetness. All these things the Apostle enumerates. "*I beseech you therefore, brethren, by the mercy of God, that you present yourselves a living sacrifice, holy, pleasing unto God, your reasonable service.*"† As I understand the Apostle he does not exhort us to offer a sacrifice strictly speaking, as though he wished our bodies to be killed and burnt, like the bodies of sheep when offered in sacrifice, but to offer a mystical and reasonable sacrifice, a sacrifice that is similar but not the same, a spiritual and not a corporal one. The Apostle therefore exhorts us to the imitation of Christ inasmuch as he offered on the Cross for our advantage the sacrifice of his body by a true and real death, so we, for His honour, should offer our bodies as a living, a holy and perfect victim, a victim which is

* Heb. xiii. 15. † Rom. xii. 1.

pleasing to GOD, and which in a spiritual manner is slain and burnt.

We will now give a few words of explanation concerning the four decrees which regulated the Jewish sacrifices. In the first place, our bodies should be victims consecrated to GOD, which we should use for the honour of GOD. For we must not look upon our bodies as our own property, but as the property of GOD, to Whom we were consecrated in Baptism, and Who has bought us at a great price, as the Apostle tells the Corinthians. Nor ought we to be merely victims, but victims living by the life of grace and of the Holy Spirit. For those who are dead by sin are not victims of GOD, but of the devil, who kills our souls and rejoices in their destruction. Our GOD, Who always was and is the fountain of life, will not have offered to Him fœtid carcases which are fit for nothing but to be thrown to the beasts. In the second place, we must take great care to preserve this life of our souls so that we may offer our "*reasonable service.*" Nor is it enough for the victim to be living. It must also be holy. "*A living*" and "*holy sacrifice,*" says St. Paul. The oblation of clean victims was a holy sacrifice. As we have said before, some quadrupeds were clean, as sheep, goats, and oxen, and some birds were clean, as turtles, sparrows, and doves. The former class of animals typify the active life, the latter the contemplative. Consequently, if those who lead an active life amongst the faithful desire to offer themselves as holy victims to GOD, they must imitate the simplicity and meekness of a sheep, which knows not revenge; the labours and seriousness of the ox, which seeks not repose, does not vainly run hither and thither, but bears its burden and drags its plough and works assiduously in the cultivation of the earth; and finally, the speed of the goat in climbing mountains and its quickness in detecting objects from afar. They must not rest satisfied with meekness only, or with undertaking certain duties. They must lift up their hearts by frequent prayer and contemplate the things which are above. For how can they perform their actions for the glory of GOD and make them ascend like the incense of sacrifice before Him, if they seldom or never think of GOD, seek Him not, and are not by means of meditation burning with His love? The active life of a Christian should not be entirely separated from the contemplative, just as the contemplative should not be entirely separated from the active. Those who do not follow the example of oxen and sheep and goats in continually and usefully labouring for their Master, but seek and pursue their own temporal commodities, cannot offer to GOD a holy victim. They resemble rather such ferocious and carnivorous beasts as wolves, dogs, bears, kites, and ravens, which make a god of their belly, and follow in the tracks of that "*roaring lion*" which "*goeth about seeking whom he may devour.*"[*] Those Christians who lead a contemplative life and desire to offer themselves as living and holy victims to GOD must imitate the solitude of the turtle, the purity of the dove, and the prudence of the sparrow. The solitude of the turtle is chiefly applicable to monks and hermits who have no communication with the world, and are wholly intent on the contemplation of GOD and singing His praises. The purity and fecundity of the dove is necessary for bishops and priests who have intercourse with men and ought to bring forth and nourish spiritual children, and it will be difficult for them to imitate such purity and fruitfulness unless they frequently fly up to their heavenly country by contemplation, and by charity condescend to succour the necessities of men. There is a danger of their wholly abandoning themselves to contemplation and being unproductive of spiritual children, or of becoming so engrossed in external work as to be

* 1 St. Peter v. 8.

contaminated with earthly desires, and whilst they are all anxiety to save the souls of others, may themselves—which GOD avert—become castaways. The prudence of the sparrow is necessary both for contemplatives as well as for those who devote themselves to the active duties of the ministry. There are both hedge-sparrows and house-sparrows. Hedge-sparrows show the greatest care in avoiding the nets and snares set for them, and house-sparrows, which dwell near men, never become the friends of man, and with difficulty are captured by men. So Christians, and especially priests and monks, must imitate the prudence of the sparrow to avoid falling into the nets and snares set for them by the devil, and when they treat with men, should do so solely for their neighbours' advantage, should avoid all familiarity with them, especially with women, should fly from idle conversations, should decline invitations, and should not be present at plays and theatres.

The last decree regarding sacrifices was that the victim should not only be living and holy but also pleasing, that is, should send forth a most sweet odour, according to what the Scriptures say: "*And the Lord smelled a sweet savour,*"* and "*Christ delivered Himself for us, an oblation and a sacrifice to God for an odour of sweetness.*"† It was necessary that the victim, in order to send forth this odour so pleasing to GOD, should be both killed and burnt. This takes place in the mystical and reasonable sacrifice of which we are speaking, when the concupiscence of the flesh is completely brought into subjection and burnt out by the fire of charity. Nothing more efficaciously, quickly, and perfectly mortifies the concupiscence of the flesh than a sincere love of GOD. For He is the King and Lord of all the affections of our heart, and all our affections are ruled by Him and depend

* Genesis viii. 21.   † Ephes. v. 2.

upon Him, whether they be those of fear or hope, or desire or hatred, or anger, or any other inquietude of mind. Now love yields to nothing except to a stronger love, and consequently when Divine love has complete possession of the heart of man and sets it wholly in flame, all carnal desires yield to it, and being completely subdued occasion us no disquiet: and, therefore, ardent aspirations and fervent prayers should ascend from our hearts like incense before the throne of GOD. This is the sacrifice which GOD demands of us, and which the Apostle exhorts us to be ever most ready to offer.

St. Paul uses a very strong argument to persuade us to it, as it is of itself so hard and full of difficulty. His argument is expressed in these words. "*I beseech you, brethren, by the mercy of God that you present your bodies a living sacrifice.*"* In the Greek text we find the word mercies used instead of mercy. What and how many are the mercies of GOD by which the Apostle beseeches us? In the first place there is creation, by which we were made something whereas before we were nothing. Secondly, although Almighty GOD stood in no need of our service, He has made us His servants, because He wishes us to do something for which He can reward us. Thirdly, He made us to His image, and rendered us capable of knowing Him and loving Him. Fourthly, He made us through Christ His adopted children and coheirs of His only Begotten Son. Fifthly, He has made us members of His Spouse, and of that Church of which He is the Head. Lastly, He offered Himself on the Cross, "*an oblation and a sacrifice to God for an odour of sweetness,*"† to redeem us from slavery and wash us from our iniquities, "*that He might present it to Himself a glorious Church not having spot or wrinkle.*"‡ These are the mercies of GOD by which the Apostle beseeches us,

* Rom. xii. 1.   † Ephes. v. 2.   ‡ Ephes. v. 27.

as if he would say: The Lord has showered so many graces upon you, who have neither deserved them nor asked for them, and should you think it a hard matter to offer yourselves as living, holy, and reasonable victims to GOD? Forsooth, far from being difficult, it should seem to anyone who attentively considers all the circumstances, light and easy and pleasant and agreeable to serve so good a GOD with our whole hearts throughout all time, and after the example of Christ to offer ourselves wholly to Him as a victim, on oblation, and a holocaust in the odour of sweetness.

CHAPTER XVI.
The fourth fruit to be drawn from the consideration of the sixth word spoken by Christ upon the Cross.

A fourth fruit can be drawn from a fourth explanation of the word "*It is finished.*" For if it is time, as most certainly it is, that GOD by the merits of Christ has withdrawn us from the servitude of the devil, and placed us in the kingdom of His Beloved Son, let us inquire and not desist from our inquiry till we have found the reason why so many men prefer the slavery of the enemy of mankind to the service of Christ, our most kind Master, and choose rather to burn for ever in the flames of hell with Satan, than reign most happy in eternal glory with our Lord JESUS CHRIST. The only reason I can find is that the service of Christ begins with the Cross. It is necessary to crucify the flesh with its vices and concupiscences. This bitter draught, this chalice of gall naturally produces a nausea in frail man, and is often the sole reason why he would rather be the slave of his passions than be the master of them by such a remedy. I would, indeed, allow a man, or rather not a man but a beast, for a man bereft of his reason is such, to be ruled by his desires and appetites: but since man is endowed with reason, he certainly knows or ought to know that he who is commanded to crucify his flesh with its vices and concupiscences should insist on keeping this precept, particularly as he is assisted by GOD'S grace to do so, and that our Lord like a wise physician so prepares this bitter potion that it may be drunk without difficulty. Moreover, if any one of us individually was the first person to whom these words were addressed, "*Take up your cross and follow Me,*" we might have an excuse for hesitating and mistrusting our own strength, and not daring to lay our hands on a cross which we considered ourselves unable to carry; but since not only men but even children of tender years have boldly taken up the Cross of Christ, have patiently carried it, and have crucified their flesh with its vices and concupiscences, why should we fear, why should we hesitate? St. Augustine was vanquished by this argument, and at once mastered his carnal concupiscence which for years he had regarded as unconquerable. He placed before the eyes of his soul many men and women who had led chaste lives, and said to himself: "Why cannot you do what so many of both sexes have done who trusted not in their own strength, but in the Lord their GOD?" What has been said about the concupiscence of the flesh, may be said with equal force about the concupiscence of the eyes—which is avarice, and the pride of life. There is no vice which with God's assistance cannot be overcome, and there is no reason to fear that GOD will refuse to help us. St. Leo says: "Almighty GOD justly insists on our keeping His commandments since He prevents us by His grace." Miserable and mad and foolish then are those souls who prefer rather to carry five yoke of oxen under the command of Satan, and with labour and sorrow be the slaves of their senses, and at last be tortured for ever with their leader, the devil, in the flames of hell, than to submit to the yoke of Christ, which is sweet and light, to find rest for their souls in this life, and in the life to come an eternal crown with their King in everlasting glory.

CHAPTER XVII.

The fifth fruit to be drawn from the consideration of the sixth word spoken by Christ upon the Cross.

A fifth fruit may be gathered from this word, since we may apply it to the building of the Church which was perfected on the Cross. The Church was formed from the side of Christ as He was expiring on the Cross, like another Eve formed from the rib of another Adam. And this mystery should teach us to love the Cross, to honour the Cross, and to be closely united to the Cross. For who does not love his mother's birthplace? All the faithful have an extraordinary veneration for the holy house of Loretto, because it is the birthplace of the Virgin Mother of GOD, and there in her virginal womb she conceived JESUS CHRIST our Lord, as the Angel announced to St. Joseph: "*For that which is conceived in her is of the Holy Ghost.*"* So the Holy Roman Church, mindful of the place of her nativity, has the Cross planted everywhere and everywhere exhibited. We are taught to make it on ourselves; we see it in churches and houses; she confers no sacrament without the Cross; blesses nothing without the sign of the Cross; and we, the children of the Church, show our love for the Cross when we patiently endure adversities for the love of our crucified GOD. This is to glory in the Cross. This is to do what the Apostles did "*when they went from the prescnce of the council rejoicing that they were accounted*

* St. Matt. i. 20.

worthy to suffer reproach for the name of Jesus." St. Paul plainly gives us to understand what he means by glorying in the Cross when he says : " *We glory also in tribulations, knowing that tribulation worketh patience, and patience trial, and trial hope, and hope confoundeth not, because the charity of God is poured forth in our hearts by the Holy Ghost, Who is given to us.*"† And again in his Epistle to the Galatians : " *God forbid that I should glory, save in the Cross of our Lord Jesus Christ, by Whom the world is crucified to me and I to the world.*" ‡ This is indeed the triumph of the Cross ; when the world with its pomps and pleasures is dead to the Christian soul that loves Christ crucified, and the soul is dead to the world by loving tribulations and contempt which the world hates, and hating the pleasures of the flesh, and the empty applause of men which the world loves. In this manner is the true servant of GOD rendered so perfect that it may also be said of him : "*It is finished.*"

CHAPTER XVIII.

The sixth fruit to be drawn from the consideration of the sixth word spoken by Christ upon the Cross.

The last fruit to be drawn from the consideration of this word is to be gathered from the perseverance which our Lord exhibited on the Cross. We are taught by this word, "*It is finished*," how our Lord so perfected the work of His Passion from the beginning to the end that nothing was wanting to it : " *The works of God are perfect.*"§ And as GOD the Father completed the work of creation on the sixth day and rested on the seventh, so the Son of GOD completed the work of our redemption

* Acts v. 41.   † Rom. v. 3—5.
‡ Gal. vi. 14.   § Deut. xxxii. 4.

on the sixth day and rested in the sleep of death on the seventh. In vain did the Jews taunt Him: "*If He be the King of Israel let Him come down from the Cross and we will believe Him.*"* With more truth does St. Bernard exclaim: "Because He is the King of Israel He will not desert the ensign of His royalty. He would not give us an excuse for failing in perseverance, which alone is crowned: He would not make the tongues of preachers dumb, nor the lips of those who console the weak mute, nor the words of those void whose duty it is to say to every one, Do not abandon your cross, for without doubt each individual soul would answer if it could: I have abandoned my cross because Christ first deserted His." Christ then persevered on His Cross even unto His death in order so to perfect His work that nothing should be wanting to it, and to leave us an example of perseverance in every way worthy of our admiration. It is easy indeed to stay in places which are agreeable to us, or to persevere in duties which are pleasant, but it is very difficult to remain at one's post where there is much grief to be allayed, or to continue in an occupation where there is much anxiety attached to it. But if we could understand the reason which induced our Lord to persevere on the Cross, we should be thoroughly convinced that we ought to bear our cross with constancy, and if need be, to bear it with courage even unto death. If we fix our eyes on the Cross alone we cannot but be filled with horror at the sight of such an instrument of death, but if we fix our eyes on Him Who bids us carry the Cross, and on the place whither the Cross will lead us, and on the fruit which the Cross will produce in us, then instead of appearing full of difficulties and obstacles, it will be easy and agreeable to persevere in carrying it, and even to remain with constancy nailed to it.

* St. Matt. xxvii. 42.

Why then did Christ hang upon His Cross with such perseverance even unto death without a sigh and without a murmur? The first reason was the love He bore His Father: "*The chalice which My Father hath given Me shall I not drink it?*"* Christ loved His Father and the Father loved His Only Begotten Son, with an equally ineffable love. And when He saw the chalice of suffering offered to Him by His all-good and all-loving Father in such a manner that He could not but conclude it was presented to Him for the best of purposes, we cannot wonder at His drinking it to the dregs with the utmost readiness. The Father had made a marriage feast for His Son, and had given Him for His Spouse the Church— disfigured and deformed indeed, but which He was lovingly to cleanse in the bath of His Precious Blood, and render beautiful, "*not having spot nor wrinkle.*"† Christ on His side dearly loved the Spouse given Him by His Father, and hesitated not to pour out His Blood to render her fair and comely. Now if Jacob toiled for seven years in feeding the flocks of Laban, suffered from heat and cold and want of sleep in order to marry Rachel, and if these seven years of labour passed so quickly that "*they seemed but a few days because of the greatness of his love,*" ‡ and a second seven years seemed equally as short, we cannot be surprised that the Son of GOD desired to hang on the Cross for three hours for His Spouse, the Church, who was to be the mother of so many thousands of saints and the parent of so many children of GOD. Moreover, in drinking the bitter chalice of His Passion, Christ was influenced not only by His love for His Father and His Spouse, but also by the exalted glory and the boundless never-ending happiness He was to secure by means of His Cross: "*He humbled Himself, becoming obedient unto death, even to*

---

* St. John xviii. 11.
† Ephes. v. 27.   ‡ Genesis xxix. 20.

the death of the Cross. *For which cause God also hath exalted Him, and hath given Him a name which is above all names: that in the name of Jesus every knee should bow, of those that are in heaven, on earth, and under the earth, and that every tongue should confess that the Lord Jesus Christ is in the glory of God the Father."* *

To the example which Christ has set us, let us add also the examples which the Apostles hold out for our imitation. St. Paul in his Epistle to the Romans, after enumerating his own crosses and those of his fellow-labourers, asks: "*Who then shall separate us from the love of Christ? shall tribulation? or distress? or famine? or nakedness? or danger? or persecution? or the sword? As it is written: For Thy sake we are put to death all the day long. We are accounted as sheep for the slaughter.*" And he answers his own questions. "*But in all these things we overcome because of Him that hath loved us.*" † We must not regard the suffering which crosses entail if we wish to persevere unflinchingly in bearing them, but rather encourage ourselves by the love of that GOD Who so loved us as to give His only Son for our ransom, or even keep our eyes fixed on that Son of GOD Who loved us and "*gave Himself for us.*" ‡ In his Epistle to the Corinthians the same Apostle says: "*I am filled with comfort. I exceedingly abound with joy in all our tribulations.*" § Whence arose this consolation and this joy which rendered him, so to speak, impassible in every affliction? He supplies us with the answer. "*For that which is at present momentary and light of our tribulation, worketh for us above measure exceedingly an eternal weight of glory.*" ‖ Thus the contemplation of the crown which awaited him, and the thought of which he ever kept before him, rendered all the trials of this life momentary

---

* Philipp. ii. 8—11. † Rom. viii. 35—37.
‡ Titus ii. 14. § 2 Cor. vii. 4. ‖ 2 Cor. iv. 17.

and trivial. "What persecution," cries out St. Cyprian, "can prevail against such thoughts as these? what torments can overcome such a vision?"* As a second model we will take the conduct of St. Andrew, who looked upon the cross, on which he was to hang for two days, not as a gibbet, but embraced it as a friend, and when the spectators of his execution wished to take him down, he would by no means consent to it, as he desired to remain fastened to his cross even to death. And this is not the action of a crazy or foolish person, but of an enlightened Apostle and of a man filled with the Holy Ghost.

All Christians can learn from the example of Christ and His Apostles how to conduct themselves when they cannot descend from their cross, that is, when they cannot free themselves from some particular affliction or suffering without sin. In the first place the life of each religious, who is bound by the vows of poverty, chastity, and obedience, is compared to a martyrdom from which he must not shrink. Again, if a husband is wedded to a wife who is quarrelsome, morose, and peevish, or a wife is married to a husband whose temper and character is not a whit the less difficult to put up with, as St. Augustine in his *Book of Confessions* assures us was the disposition of his father, the husband of St. Monica, the cross must courageously be borne as the bond is indissoluble. Slaves who have lost their liberty, prisoners condemned to a life-long servitude, the sick who are suffering from an incurable disease, the poor who are tempted to secure a momentary relief by theft or robbery, each and all must turn their thoughts, not to the cross they are carrying, but to Him Who has placed the cross upon them, if they wish to persevere in carrying it with internal peace, and desire to gain the immense reward which is promised to them in heaven when their sufferings here shall be over.

* Cyprian, *Lib. de Exhort. Martyr.*

Without doubt it is GOD Who afflicts us with crosses, and He is our most loving Father, and without His concurrence neither sorrow nor joy can befall us. Without doubt, too, whatever happens to us by His will is the best for us, and ought to be so agreeable to us as to force us to say with Christ: "*The chalice which My Father has given Me shall I not drink it?*"* and with the Apostle: "*But in all these things we overcome because of Him that hath loved us.*" † Consequently those who cannot lay aside their cross without sin must consider not their present suffering, but the crown which awaits them, and the possession of which will more than counterbalance all the afflictions, all the griefs of this life. "*For I reckon that the sufferings of this time are not worthy to be compared with the glory to come that shall be revealed in us,*" ‡ is what St. Paul said of himself, and the judgment he passed on Moses was: "*Rather choosing to be afflicted with the people of God, than to have the pleasure of sin for a time, esteeming the reproach of Christ greater riches than the treasure of the Egyptians. For He looked unto the reward.*" §

For the consolation of those who are forced to bear the heavy weight of a cross through a long series of years, it will not be out of place briefly to relate the story of two souls who failed to persevere, and found a far heavier and eternal cross awaiting them. When the traitor Judas began to reflect upon and detest the enormity of his treachery, he felt unable to bear the shame and confusion of again meeting any one of the Apostles or disciples of Christ, and he hanged himself with a halter. Far from escaping the shame which he dreaded, he has only exchanged one cross for a heavier one. For his confusion will be much greater when at the Day of Judgment he will have to stand before all angels and men, not only

* St. John xviii. 11.   † Rom. viii. 37.
‡ Rom. viii. 18.   § Heb. xi. 25, 26.

as the convicted betrayer of his Master, but also as a self-murderer. What folly it was on his part to avoid a little shame before the then little flock of Christ, who would all have been meek and kind towards him like their Master, and would all have had him trust in the mercy of his Redeemer, and not to have avoided the infamy and the ignominy which he must suffer when he stands forth in the sight of all creatures as a traitor to his GOD and a suicide. The other example is taken from the panegyric of St. Basil on the forty martyrs. In the persecution of the Emperor Licinius, forty soldiers were condemned to death for their steadfast belief in Christ. They were ordered to be exposed naked during the night on a frozen lake, and to gain their crown by the slow agony of being frozen to death. Beside the frozen lake there was prepared a hot bath, into which any one who denied his faith had liberty to plunge. Thirty-nine of the martyrs turned their thoughts to the eternal happiness which awaited them, regarded not their present suffering which would soon be over, persevered with ease in their faith, and deserved to receive from the hands of JESUS CHRIST their crown of everlasting glory. But one pondered and brooded over his torments, could not persevere, and plunged into the hot bath beside him. As the blood began to flow again through his frozen limbs, he breathed forth his soul, which, branded with the disgrace of being a denier of its GOD, forthwith descended to the eternal torments of hell. By seeking to avoid death, this unhappy wretch found it, and exchanged a transitory and comparatively light cross for one which is unbearable and eternal. The imitators of these two miserable men are to be found among those who abandon their religious life, who cast from them the yoke which is sweet and the burden which is light, and when they least expect it, find themselves bound as slaves to the heavier yoke of their various appetites which they can never satisfy, and pressed down under the galling burden of innumerable sins. Those who refuse to carry the Cross of Christ, are obliged to carry the bonds and the chains of Satan.

CHAPTER XIX.

The literal explanation of the seventh word, " Father, into Thy hands I commend My spirit."

We have come to the last word which our Lord pronounced. At the point of death JESUS *"crying with a loud voice said: Father, into Thy hands I commend my spirit."* * We will explain each word separately. *"Father."* Deservedly does He call GOD His Father, for He was a Son who had been obedient to His Father even unto death, and it was proper that His last dying bequest, which was certain to be heard, should be prefaced by such a tender name. *"Into Thy Hands."* In the Sacred Scriptures the hands of GOD signify the intelligence and the will of GOD, or in other words His wisdom and power; or, again, the intelligence of GOD which knows all things, and the will of GOD which can do all things. With these two attributes as with hands, GOD does all things, and stands not in need of any instruments in the accomplishment of His will. St. Leo says: "The will of GOD is His omnipotence."† Consequently, with GOD to will is to do. *"He hath done all things, whatsoever He would."*‡ *"I commend."* I hand over to your keeping My life, with the sure faith of its being restored when the time of My resurrection shall come. *"My spirit."* There is a diversity of opinion as to the meaning of this word. Ordinarily the word spirit is synonymous with soul, which is the substantial form of the body, but it can also mean life itself, since breathing is the

* St. Luke xxiii. 46.   † Serm. ii. *De Nativ.*   ‡ Psalm cxiii. 3.

sign of life. Those who breathe live, and those die who cease to breathe. If by the word spirit we here understand the soul of Christ, we must take care not to think that His soul at the moment of its separation from the body was in any danger. We are accustomed to commend with many prayers and much anxiety the souls of the agonizing, because they are on the point of appearing at the tribunal of a strict Judge to receive the reward or the punishment of their thoughts, words, and deeds. The soul of Christ was in no such need, both because it enjoyed the beatific vision from the time of its creation, was hypostatically united to the person of the Son of GOD, and could even be called the soul of GOD, and also because victorious and triumphant it was leaving the body an object of terror to the devils, not a soul to be scared by them. If the word spirit then is to be taken as synonymous with soul, the meaning of these words of our Lord, "*I commend my spirit*," is that the soul of Christ which was enclosed in the body as in a tabernacle was about to throw itself into the hands of the Father as into a place of trust until it should return to the body, according to the words of the Book of Wisdom: "*The souls of the just are in the hand of God.*"* However, the more generally accepted meaning of the word in this passage is the life of the body. With this interpretation the word may be thus amplified. I now give up My breath of life, and as I cease to breathe I cease to live. But this breath, this life I intrust to you, my Father, that in a short time you may again restore it to My body. In your keeping nothing perishes. In you all things live. By a word you call into existence things which were not, and by a word you give life to those who had it not.

We may gather that this is the true interpretation of the word from the thirtieth Psalm, one of the verses of

* Wisdom iii. 1.

which our Lord was quoting: "*Thou wilt bring me out of this snare which they have hidden for me, for Thou art my protector. Into Thy hands I commend my spirit.*"* In this verse the Prophet clearly means to signify life by the word spirit, since he beseeches GOD to preserve his life, and not to suffer him to be killed by his enemies. If we consider the context in the Gospel, it is clear that this is the meaning our Lord also intended to convey. For after he had said, "*Father, into Thy hands I commend My spirit,*" the Evangelist adds: "*And saying this He gave up the Ghost.*"† Now to expire is the same as to cease breathing, which is the characteristic of those only who live. It cannot be said of the soul, which is the substantial form of the body, as it can of the air we inhale, that we breathe it as long as we live, and we cease breathing it as soon as we die. Lastly, our interpretation is strengthened by the words of St. Paul: "*Who in the days of His flesh with a strong cry and tears offering up prayers and supplications to Him that was able to save Him from death, was heard for His reverence.*"‡ Some authors refer this passage to our Lord's prayer in the Garden: "*Abba, Father, all things are possible to Thee, remove this chalice from Me.*"§ But the reference is incorrect, as our Lord on that occasion neither prayed with a loud cry, nor was His prayer heard, and He Himself did not wish to be heard in order to be delivered from death. He prayed that the chalice of His Passion might pass from Him to show His natural repugnance to death, and to prove He was really man whose nature it is to dread its approach. And after this prayer he added: "*But not what I will, but what Thou wilt.*"‖ Consequently the prayer in the Garden was not the prayer to which the Apostle alludes in his Epistle to the Hebrews. Others, again, refer this text of St. Paul to the prayer which Christ made on the

---

* Psalm xxx. 5, 6.   † St. Luke xxiii. 46.   ‡ Heb. v. 7.
§ St. Mark xiv. 36.   ‖ St. Mark xiv. 36.

Cross for those who were crucifying Him. "*Father, forgive them, for they know not what they do.*"* On that occasion, however, our Lord did not pray with a loud cry, and He did not pray for Himself, neither did he pray to be delivered from death, and both these objects the Apostle distinctly mentions as being the ends of our Lord's prayer. It remains then, that the words of St. Paul must refer to the prayer Christ made with His dying breath: "*Father, into Thy hands I commend my spirit.*"† This prayer, St. Luke says, he gave forth with a loud voice: "*And Jesus crying with a loud voice, said.*" The words of both St. Paul and St. Luke agree in this interpretation. Moreover, as St. Paul says, our Lord prayed to be saved from death, and this cannot mean that He prayed to be saved from death on the Cross, for in that case His prayer was not heard, and the Apostle assures us it was heard. The true meaning is that He prayed not to be swallowed up by death, but merely to taste death and then return to life again. This is the evident explanation of the words: "*With a strong cry and tears offering up prayers and supplications to Him that was able to save Him from death.*"‡ Our Lord could not but know that He must die as He was already so near death, and He desired to be delivered from death in the sense only of not being held captive by death. In other words, he prayed for His speedy resurrection, and this' prayer was readily granted, as He rose again triumphant on the third day. This interpretation of the passage of St. Paul proves beyond doubt that when our Lord said: "*Into Thy hands I commend my spirit,*" the word spirit is synonymous with life and not with the soul. Our Lord was not anxious about His soul, which He knew to be in safety, as it already enjoyed the beatific vision, and had beheld its God face to face from the moment of its creation, but He was anxious for His

* St. Luke xxiii. 34. † St. Luke xxiii. 46. ‡ Heb. v. 7.

body, which He foresaw would soon be deprived of life, and He prayed that His body might not long be kept in the sleep of death. This prayer was tenderly listened to and abundantly.

CHAPTER XX.

The first fruit to be drawn from the consideration of the seventh word spoken by Christ upon the Cross.

According to the practice we have so far pursued, we will gather a few fruits from the consideration of the last word spoken by Christ on the Cross, and from His death, which immediately followed. And first we will show the wisdom, the power, and the infinite charity of GOD from the very circumstance which seems attended with such weakness and folly. His power is clearly shown in this, that our Lord died whilst He was crying out with a loud voice. From this we conclude that had it been His will He need not have died, but He died because He willed. As a rule, people at the point of death gradually lose their strength and voice, and at the last gasp are not able to articulate. And so it was not without reason that the Centurion, on hearing such a loud cry proceed from the lips of Christ, Who had lost almost every drop of blood in His veins, exclaimed: "*Indeed, this was the Son of God.*"*
Christ is a mighty Lord, inasmuch as He showed His power even in His death, not only by crying aloud with His last breath, but also by making the earth tremble, by splitting rocks asunder, by opening graves, and rending the veil of the Temple. We know, on the authority of St. Matthew, that all these things happened at the death of Christ, and each and all of these events has its hidden meaning wherein is manifested His Divine wisdom. The earthquake and the splitting of the rocks showed that His

* St. Matt. xxvii. 54.

death and Passion would move men to penance and would soften the hardest hearts. St. Luke gives this interpretation to these mysterious omens, for after having mentioned them he adds, that the Jews returned from the sight of the Crucifixion *"striking their breasts."** The opening of the graves foreshadowed the glorious resurrection of the dead, which was one of the results of the death of Christ. The rending of the veil of the Temple, whereby the Holy of Holies could be seen, was a pledge that heaven would be opened by the merits of His death and Passion, and that all the predestined should there behold GOD face to face. Nor was His wisdom exhibited merely in these signs and wonders. It was exhibited also by producing life out of death, as was prefigured by Moses producing water from the rock,† and by the simile in which Christ compared Himself to a grain of wheat.‡ For as it is necessary for the seed to be crushed in order to produce the ear of corn, so by His death on the Cross Christ enriched a countless multitude of all nations in the life of grace. St. Peter expresses the same idea when he speaks of JESUS CHRIST as *"swallowing down death that we might be made heirs of life everlasting."*§ As though he would say: The first man tasted the forbidden fruit and subjected all his posterity to death; the Second Man tasted the bitter fruit of death, and all who are born again in Him receive everlasting life. Lastly, His wisdom was manifested in the manner of His death, as from that moment the Cross, than which previously nothing was more ignominious and disgraceful, became an emblem so dignified and glorious that even kings consider it an honour to wear it as an ornament. In her admiration of the Cross the Church sings—

> Sweet are the nails, and sweet the wood,
> That bears a weight so sweet and good.

* St. Luke xxiii. 48.   † Numb. xx. 11.   ‡ St. John xii. 24.
§ 1 Peter iii. 22.

St. Andrew, on beholding the cross on which he was to be crucified, exclaimed: "Hail, precious cross, that hast been adorned by the precious limbs of my Lord. Long have I desired thee, ardently have I sought thee, uninterruptedly have I loved thee, and now I find thee ready to receive my longing soul. Secure and full of joy I come to thee, and do thou receive me into thy embrace, for I am the disciple of Christ my Lord, Who redeemed me by hanging upon thee."

Now what shall we say of the infinite charity of GOD. Previous to His death our Lord said: "*Greater love than this no man hath, that a man lay down his life for his friends.*"* Christ literally laid down His life, for against His will no one could deprive Him of it. "*No man taketh it away from Me; but I lay it down of Myself.*"† A man cannot show greater love for his friends than by giving his life for them, since nothing is more precious or dearer than life, as it is the foundation of every happiness. "*For what doth it profit a man if he gain the whole world and suffer the loss of his own soul,*"‡ that is, his life. Each one instinctively repels with all his strength an attack made upon his life. We read in Job: "*Skin for skin, and all that a man hath will he give for his life.*"§ So far, however, we have looked upon this fact in a general way; we will now descend to particulars. In many ways, and in an ineffable manner, Christ showed His love towards the whole human race, and to each individual, by dying on the Cross. In the first place, His life was the most precious of all lives, since it was the life of the Man-GOD, the life of the most mighty of Kings, the life of the wisest of Doctors, the life of the best of men. In the second place He laid down this life for His enemies, for sinners, for ungrateful wretches. Moreover, He laid down His life in order that at the price

---

* St. John xv. 13. † St. John x. 18. ‡ St. Matt. xvi. 26.
§ Job ii. 4.

of His own blood, these enemies of His, these sinners, these ungrateful wretches, should be snatched from the flames of hell. And lastly, He laid down His life to make these enemies, these sinners, these ungrateful wretches, His brothers, co-heirs and joint possessors with Him of eternal happiness in the kingdom of heaven. Shall there now be one soul so callous and so ungrateful as not to love CHRIST JESUS with its whole heart? Shall there be one Christian soul unwilling to bear any affliction to secure His grace and live. O GOD, turn our hardened stony hearts to Thee, and not our hearts only, but the hearts of all Christians, the hearts of all men, even the hearts of infidels who have never known Thee, and of atheists who have denied Thee.

CHAPTER XXI.

The second fruit to be drawn from the consideration of the seventh word spoken by Christ upon the Cross.

Another and most profitable fruit would be gathered from the consideration of this word if we could form the habit of frequently repeating to ourselves the prayer which Christ our Master taught us on the Cross with His dying breath: "*Into Thy hands I commend my spirit.*"* Our Lord was under no such necessity as we are for making such a prayer. He was the Son of GOD and the Most Holy; we are servants and sinners, and consequently our holy Mother and Mistress the Church, teaches us to make a constant use of this prayer, and to repeat not only the part which our Lord used, but the whole of it as it is found in the Psalms of David: "*Into Thy hands I commend my spirit: Thou hast redeemed me O Lord, the God of truth.*"† Our Lord omitted the last part of the verse because He

* St. Luke xxiii. 46. † Psalm xxx. 6.

was the Redeemer and not one of the redeemed, but we who have been redeemed with His precious Blood must not omit it. Moreover, Christ, as the Only Begotten Son of GOD, prayed to His Father, we, on the other hand, pray to Christ as our Redeemer, and consequently we do not say: "*Father, into Thy hands I commend my spirit,*" but, "*Into Thy hands, O Lord, I commend my spirit; Thou hast redeemed me O Lord, the God of truth.*" The Protomartyr St. Stephen was the first to use this prayer when at the point of death he exclaimed: "*Lord Jesus, receive my spirit.*"*

Our holy Mother the Church teaches us to make use of this ejaculation on three different occasions. She teaches us to say it daily at the beginning of Complin, as those who recite the Divine Office can bear me out. Secondly, when we approach the Holy Eucharist, after the *Domine non sum dignus*, the priest says first for himself and then for the other communicants. "*Into Thy hands, O Lord, I commend my spirit.*" Lastly, at the point of death, she recommends all the faithful to imitate their dying Lord in the use of this prayer. There can be no doubt that we are ordered to say this versicle at Complin, because that part of the Divine Office is recited at the end of the day, and St. Basil in his rules explains how easy it is when darkness first comes on, and night sets in to commend our spirit to GOD, so that if a sudden death overtake us we may not be found unprepared. The reason why the same ejaculation should be used at the moment we receive the Blessed Eucharist is clear, for the reception of the Blessed Eucharist is perilous and at the same time so necessary that we cannot approach too often nor altogether absent ourselves without danger: "*Whoever shall eat this bread, or drink the chalice of the Lord unworthily, shall be guilty of the Body and of the Blood of our Lord,*" and "*eateth and drinketh*

---

* Acts vii. 58.

*judgment to himself."** And he who does not receive the Body of Christ our Lord does not receive the bread of life, even life itself. So we are surrounded with perils like starved and famished men who are uncertain whether the food that is offered them is poisoned or not. With fear and trembling then ought we to exclaim: Lord, I am not worthy that Thou shouldst enter under my roof, unless Thou in Thy goodness makest me worthy, and therefore say only the word and my soul shall be healed. But since I have reason to doubt whether Thou wouldst deign to heal my wounds, I commend my spirit into Thy hands, so that in an affair of such moment Thou mayest be near and assist my soul which Thou hast redeemed with Thy precious Blood.

If some Christians would seriously think of these things they would not be so eager to receive the priesthood with the object of gaining their livelihood from the stipends they receive for their Masses. Such priests are not as anxious to approach this great Sacrifice with a fitting preparation, as they are anxious to obtain the end they propose to themselves, which is to secure food for their bodies and not for their souls. There are others also, attendants at the palaces of prelates or princes, who approach this tremendous mystery through human respect, lest perchance they should incur the displeasure of their masters by not communicating at the regularly constituted times. What then is to be done? Is it more advantageous seldom to approach this Divine Banquet? Certainly not. Far better is it to approach often but with due preparation, for, as St. Cyril says, the less often we approach the less prepared are we to receive the heavenly manna.

The approach of death is a time when it behoves us with great ardour to repeat over and over again the prayer: *" Into Thy hands, O Lord, I commend my spirit; Thou hast*

---
* 1 Cor. xi. 27, 29.

redeemed me, O Lord, the God of truth." For if our soul when it leaves the body falls into the hands of Satan, there is no hope of salvation; if, on the contrary, it falls into the paternal hands of GOD, there is no longer any cause for fearing the power of our enemy. Consequently with intense grief, with true and perfect contrition, with unbounded confidence in the infinite mercy of our GOD we must at that dread moment over and over again cry out: *"Into Thy hands, O Lord, I commend my spirit."* And as in that last moment, those who during life thought little of GOD are most severely tempted to despair, because they have now no longer time for repentance, they must take up the shield of faith, by remembering that it is written, *"The wickedness of the wicked shall not hurt him in what day soever he shall turn from his wickedness,"** and the helmet of hope, by trusting in the goodness and compassion of GOD, and continually repeat, *"Into Thy hands, O Lord, I commend my spirit,"* nor fail to add that part of the prayer which is the foundation of our hope, *"for Thou hast redeemed us, O Lord, the God of truth."* Who can give back to JESUS CHRIST the innocent blood He has shed for us? Who can repay the ransom with which He purchased us? St. Augustine, in the ninth book of his Confessions, encourages each Christian soul to place unlimited confidence in our Redeemer, because the work of redemption being once accomplished can never be useless or invalid, unless we place an unsurmountable barrier to its effect by our impenitence and despair.

* Ezech. xxxiii. 12.

Chapter XXII.

The third fruit to be drawn from the consideration of the seventh word spoken by Christ upon the Cross.

The third fruit to be gathered is this. At the approach of death we must not rely too much on the alms, the fastings, and the prayers of our relations and friends. Many during life forget all about their souls and think of nothing else and do nothing else than heap up money so that their children or nephews may abound in riches. When death approaches they begin for the first time to think of their own souls, and as they have left all their wordly substance to their relatives, they also commend to them their souls to be assisted by their alms, their prayers, the Sacrifice of the Mass, and other good works. The example of Christ does not teach us to act in this manner. He commended His spirit not to His relations but to His Father. St. Peter does not tell us to act in this manner, but to "*commend*" our "*souls in good deeds to the faithful Creator.*"*

I do not find fault with those who order or seek or desire that alms should be given and the holy Sacrifice offered for the repose of their souls, but I blame those who place too much confidence in the prayers of their children and relatives, since experience shows us the dead are soon forgotten. I complain also that in an affair of such moment as eternal salvation Christians should not work for themselves, should not themselves bestow their alms, and secure friends by whom according to the Gospel they may be received "*into everlasting dwellings.*"† Lastly I severely reprehend those who do not obey the Prince of the Apostles who orders us to commend our souls to

---
* 1 St. Peter iv. 19. † St. Luke xvi. 9.

our faithful Creator not by our words only but by our good deeds. The deeds which will be of advantage to us in the sight of GOD are those which efficaciously and truly render us pious Christians. Let us listen to the voice from heaven which sounded in the ears of St. John: "*And I heard a voice from heaven, saying to me: Write, blessed are the dead who die in the Lord. From henceforth now, saith the Spirit, that they may rest from their labours: for their works follow them.*"* The good works therefore that are done whilst we are living, and not those which are done for us after death by our children and relatives, are the good works which will follow us, particularly if they are not only good in themselves, but, as St. Peter not without a hidden meaning expresses it, are well done. Many can enumerate countless good works of their own —many sermons, daily Masses, recitation of the Divine Office for years, the annual fast of Lent, frequent almsgiving; but when these are weighed in the divine scales, and there is a rigid scrutiny whether they have been well done, with a right intention, with due devotion, at their proper time and place, with a heart full of gratitude to GOD, oh, how many things which appeared meritorious will turn to our detriment? how many things which to the judgment of men appeared gold and silver and precious stones will be found to be wood and straw and stubble fit only for the fire? This consideration alarms me not a little, and the nearer I approach death, for the Apostle warns me, "*That which decayeth and groweth old is near its end,*"† the clearer do I see the necessity of following the advice of St. John Chrysostom. That holy doctor tells us not to think much of our good works, because if they are really good, that is well performed, they are written by GOD in the book of life, and there is no danger of our being defrauded of our just merits, but he encourages us

* Apoc. xiv. 13. † Heb. viii. 13.

to think rather of our evil deeds, and endeavour to make atonement for them with a contrite heart and a humble spirit, with many tears and serious penance.* Those who follow this advice may exclaim with great confidence at the moment of death: "*Into Thy hands, O Lord, I commend my spirit: Thou hast redeemed me, O Lord, the God of truth.*"

CHAPTER XXIII.

The fourth fruit to be drawn from the consideration of the seventh word spoken by Christ upon the Cross.

There follows a fourth fruit to be gathered from the most happy manner in which this prayer of JESUS CHRIST was heard, which should animate us to greater fervour in commending our spirits to GOD. With great truth does the Apostle say that our Lord JESUS CHRIST "*was heard for His reverence.*"† Our Lord prayed to His Father, as we have shown above, for the speedy resurrection of His body. The prayer was granted, for the resurrection was not prolonged longer than was necessary to establish the fact that the body of our Lord was really separated from His soul. Unless it could be proved that His body had been really deprived of life, the resurrection and the structure of Christian faith which is built upon that mystery would fall to the ground. Christ ought to have laid in the tomb for at least forty hours to accomplish the sign of the Prophet Jonas which He Himself said was a figure of His own death. In order that the resurrection of Christ might be hastened as much as possible, and that it might be evident His prayer had been heard, the three days and the three nights which Jonas spent in the whale's belly, were as regards the resurrection of Christ reduced to one

* Hom. xxxviii. *Ad Popul. Antioch.* † Heb. v. 7.

full day and parts of two other days. So the time our Lord's body was in the tomb cannot properly, but by a figure of speech only, be called three days and three nights. GOD the Father not only heard the prayer of Christ by accelerating the time of His resurrection, but by giving to His dead body a life incomparably better than it enjoyed before. Before His death the life of Christ was mortal; the life restored to Him was immortal. Before His death the life of Christ was passible, and subject to hunger and thirst, fatigue and wounds; the life restored to Him was impassible. Before His death the life of Christ was corporeal; the life restored to Him was spiritual, and the body was so subject to the spirit that in the twinkling of an eye it could be borne wherever the soul wished.

The Apostle gives the reason why the prayer of Christ was so readily granted by saying that "*He was heard for His reverence.*" The Greek word conveys the idea of reverential fear which was a distinguishing trait of the regard which Christ felt for His Father. Thus Isaias in enumerating the gifts of the Holy Ghost which were to adorn the soul of Christ says: "*And the Spirit of the Lord shall rest upon Him, the spirit of wisdom and of understanding, the spirit of counsel and of fortitude, the spirit of knowledge and of godliness, and He shall be filled with the spirit of the fear of the Lord.*" * In proportion as the soul of Christ was filled with a reverential fear for His Father, the Father was filled with complacency in His Son: "*This is My beloved Son, in Whom I am well pleased.*" † And as the Son reverenced the Father, so the Father ever heard His prayer and granted what He asked.

It follows then that if we desire to be heard by our Heavenly Father, and have our prayers granted, we must imitate Christ in approaching our Father Who is in heaven

* Isaias xi. 2, 3. † St. Matt. xvii. 5.

with great reverence, and prefer His honour before all things else. It will thus come to pass that our petitions will be heard, and especially the one on which our lot for eternity depends, that at the approach of death GOD should preserve our souls which have been commended to His keeping from the roaring lion which is standing ready to receive its prey. Let no one think, however, that reverence to God is shown merely in genuflections, in uncovering the head, and such external marks of worship and honour. In addition to all this, reverential fear implies a great dread of offending the Divine Majesty, an intimate and continual horror of sin not from the fear of punishment but from the love of God. He was endowed with this reverential fear who dared not even to think of sinning against GOD: "*Blessed is the man that feareth the Lord, he shall delight exceedingly in His commandments.*"* Such a man truly fears GOD, and may consequently be called blessed, since he strives to observe all His commandments. The holy widow Judith "*was greatly renowned among all because she feared the Lord very much.*"† She was both young and rich but never gave or yielded to any occasion of sin. She remained with her maidens secluded in her chamber, and "*wore hair-cloth upon her loins, and fasted every day except on the feasts of the House of Israel.*"‡ Behold with what zeal, even under the Old Law, which allowed greater freedom than the Gospel, a young and rich woman avoided sins of the flesh and for no other reason than "*because she feared the Lord very much.*" The sacred Scripture mentions the same of holy Job who made a compact with his eyes not to look at a virgin, that is, he would not look at a virgin lest any shadow of an impure thought should cross his mind. Why did holy Job take such precautions? "*I made a covenant with my eyes that I would not so much as think upon a*

* Psalm cxi. 1. † Judith viii. 8. ‡ Judith viii. 6.

*virgin. For what part should God from above have in me, and what inheritance the Almighty from on high?"** Which means that if any impure thought should defile him he would no longer be the inheritance of GOD, nor would GOD be his portion. If I wished to mention the examples of the saints of the New Law I should never finish. This, then, is the reverential fear of the saints. If we were filled with the same fear there would be nothing which we could not easily obtain from our heavenly Father.

CHAPTER XXIV.

The last fruit to be drawn from the consideration of the seventh word spoken by Christ upon the Cross.

The last fruit is drawn from the consideration of the obedience shown by Christ in His last words and in His death upon the Cross. The words of the Apostle: "*He humbled Himself, becoming obedient unto death, even the death of the Cross,*"† received their complete fulfilment when our Lord expired with these words upon His lips: "*Father, into Thy hands I commend My spirit.*" In order to gather the most precious fruit from the tree of the holy cross it must be our endeavour to examine everything that can be said about the obedience of Christ. He, the Master and the Pattern of every virtue tendered to His heavenly Father an obedience so ready and so perfect as to render it impossible to imagine or conceive anything greater.

In the first place, the obedience of Christ to His Father began with His Conception and continued uninterruptedly to His death. The life of our Lord JESUS CHRIST was one perpetual act of obedience. The soul of Christ from the moment of its creation enjoyed the exercise of its free

* Job xxxi. 1, 2.　　† Philipp. ii. 8.

will, was full of grace and wisdom, and consequently, even when inclosed in His Mother's womb, was capable of practising the virtue of obedience. The Psalmist speaking in the Person of Christ says: "*In the head of the book it is written of Me that I should do Thy will. O my God, I have desired it, and Thy law in the midst of My heart.*"* These words may be thus simplified: "*In the head of the book*—that is from the beginning to the end of the inspired writings of Scripture—it is shown that I was chosen and sent into the world "*to do Thy will. O my God, I have desired it*, and freely accepted it. I have placed "*Thy law*," Thy commandment, Thy desire, "*in the midst of My heart*," to ponder upon it constantly, to obey it accurately and promptly. The very words of Christ Himself mean the same. "*My meat is to do the will of Him that sent Me, that I may perfect His work.*"† For as a man does not take food now and again and at distant intervals during life, but daily eats and feels a pleasure in it, so Christ our Lord was intent upon being obedient to His Father every day of His life. It was His joy and His pleasure. "*I came down from heaven not to do My own will, but the will of Him that sent Me.*"‡ And again. "*He that sent Me is with Me, and He hath not left Me alone; for I do always the things that please Him.*"§ And since obedience is the most excellent of all sacrifices, as Samuel told Saul,∥ so every action which Christ performed during His life was a sacrifice most pleasing to the Divine Majesty. The first prerogative then of our Lord's obedience is that it lasted from the moment of His Conception to His Death upon the Cross.

In the second place, the obedience of Christ was not confined to one particular kind of duty, as is sometimes the case with other men, but it extended to everything

---

* Psalm xxxix. 8, 9.   † St. John iv. 34.   ‡ St. John vi. 38.
§ St. John viii. 29.   ∥ 1 Kings xv. 22.

L

which it pleased the Eternal Father to order. From this arose the many vicissitudes in our Lord's life. At one time we see Him in the desert neither eating nor drinking, perhaps even depriving Himself of sleep, and living "*with the beasts.*"* At another time we see Him mixing up with men, eating and drinking with them. Now He is living in obscurity and silence at Nazareth. Now He appears before the world endowed with eloquence and wisdom, and working miracles. On one occasion He exerts His authority and drives those from the temple who were defiling it by bartering within its precincts. On another occasion He hides Himself, and like a weak powerless man withdraws from the crowd. All these different actions required a soul devoid of self, and devoted to the will of another. Unless He had previously set the example of renouncing everything which human nature cherishes He would not have said to His disciples: "*If any man will come after Me let him deny himself,*"† let him give up his own will, renounce his own judgment. Unless He had been prepared to lay down His life with such willingness as to make it appear He really hated it, He would not have encouraged His disciples with such words as, "*If any man come to Me, and hate not his father and mother, and wife and children, and brethren and sisters, yea and His own life also, he cannot be My disciple.*"‡ This renunciation of self, which was so conspicuous in our Lord's character, is the true root and, as it were, mother of obedience, and those who are not prepared for this self-sacrifice will never acquire the perfection of obedience. How can a man promptly obey the will of another if he prefers his own will and judgment to that of another? The vast orbs of heaven obey the laws of nature both in their rising and in their setting. The angels are obedient to the will of GOD. They have no

* St. Mark i. 13.   † St. Matt. xvi. 24.   ‡ St. Luke xiv. 26.

will of their own in opposition to that of GOD, but are happily united with GOD, and are one spirit with Him. And so the Psalmist sings: "*Bless the Lord, all ye His angels: you that are mighty in strength and execute His word, hearkening to the voice of His orders.*"*

In the third place, the obedience of Christ was not only infinite in its length and breadth, but in proportion as by suffering it was humble in the lowest degree, so as to its reward is it exalted. The third characteristic then of the obedience of Christ is that it was tried by suffering and humiliations. To accomplish the will of His heavenly Father, the Infant Christ, with the full use of every faculty, consented to be inclosed for nine months in the dark prison of His Mother's womb. Other infants feel not this privation as they have not the use of reason, but Christ had the use of reason and must have dreaded the confinement in the narrow womb even of her whom He had chosen to be His Mother. Through obedience to His Father, and from the love He bore to man He overcame this dread, and the Church says: *When Thou didst take upon Thee to deliver Man, Thou didst not abhor the Virgin's womb.* Again, our dear Lord needed no small amount of patience and humility to assume the manners and the weaknesses of a child when He was not only wiser than Solomon, but was the Man "*in Whom are hid all the treasures of wisdom and knowledge.*"† Consider, moreover, what must have been His forbearance and meekness, His patience and humility, to have remained for eighteen years, from His twelfth to His thirtieth year, hidden in an obscure house at Nazareth, to have been regarded as the son of a carpenter, to have been called a carpenter, to have been thought an ignorant uneducated man, when at the same time His wisdom surpassed that of all angels and men together. During His public life He acquired great

* Psalm cii. 20. † Coloss. ii. 3.

renown by His preaching and miracles, but He suffered great wants and endured many hardships. "*The foxes have holes, and the birds of the air nests, but the Son of Man hath not where to lay His head.*"* Footsore and fatigued He would sit Himself down at the side of a well. And yet He could easily have surrounded Himself with an abundance of all things by the ministry of men or angels, had He not been restrained by the obedience He owed His Father. Shall I dwell on the contradictions He suffered, on the insults He endured, on the calumnies which were spoken against Him, on the scourges and the crown of thorns of His Passion, on the ignominy of the Cross itself? His humble obedience has taken such deep root that we can only wonder at it and admire it; we cannot perfectly imitate it.

There is yet a deeper depth to His obedience. The obedience of Christ finally reached this stage, that with a loud voice He cried out: "*Father, into Thy hands I commend My spirit. And saying this He gave up the ghost.*"† It would appear that the Son of GOD wished to address His Father in this wise: "*This commandment have I received of you, My Father,*"‡ to lay down My life in order to receive it again from your hands. The time has now come for Me to execute this last commandment of yours. And although the separation of My Soul and Body will be a bitter separation, because from the moment of their creation they have remained united in great peace and love, and although death found an entrance into this world through the malice of the devil, and human nature rebels against death, nevertheless Thy commandment is fixed deep in the inmost recesses of My Heart, and shall prevail even over death itself. Therefore am I prepared to taste the bitterness of death, and drink to the dregs the chalice you have prepared for Me. But as it is your wish

* St. Luke ix. 58.   † St. Luke xxiii. 46.   ‡ St. John x. 18.

that I should lay down My life in such a manner as to receive it back again from you, so "*into your hands I commend My spirit*," in order that you may restore it to Me at your pleasure. And then, having received His Father's permission to die, He bowed down His Head in token of His obedience, and gave up the ghost. His obedience conquered and prevailed. Not only did it receive its reward in the Person of Christ, Who, because He humbled Himself beneath all, and obeyed all for the sake of His Father, has been assumed into heaven, and from His throne there governs and rules all, but it has its reward also in this, that all who imitate Christ shall ascend the highest heavens, shall be placed as masters over all the goods of their Lord, and shall be sharers of His royal dignity and possessors of His kingdom for ever. On the other hand, the virtue of obedience has gained such a signal victory over rebellious, disobedient, and proud souls, as to make them tremble and fly from the sight of the Cross of Christ.

Whosoever desires to attain to the glory of heaven, and to find true peace and rest for his soul, must imitate the example of Christ. Not only religious who have bound themselves by a vow of obedience to their Superior, who holds the place of GOD in their regard, but all men who wish to be the disciples and brothers of Christ must aspire to gain this signal victory over themselves, otherwise they will be miserable for ever with the proud demons of hell. Inasmuch as obedience is a divine precept, and has been imposed upon all, it is necessary for all. To all without exception were the words of Christ addressed: "*Take up My yoke upon you.*"* To all preachers of the Gospel does He say: "*Obey your prelates and be subject to them.*"† To all kings does Samuel say: "*Doth the Lord desire holocausts and victims, and not rather that the Voice of the Lord should*

---

* St. Matt. xi. 29. † Heb. xiii. 17.

be obeyed? For obedience is better than sacrifices."* And to show the enormity of the sin of disobedience he added: "*Because it is like the sin of witchcraft to rebel*" against the commands of the Lord, or the commands of those who hold the place of the Lord.

For the sake of those who voluntarily devote themselves to the practice of obedience, and submit their wills to that of their Superior, I will say a few words on their happy state of life. The Prophet Jeremias, inspired by the Holy Ghost, says: "*It is good for a man, when he hath borne the yoke from his youth. He shall sit solitary and hold his peace, because he hath taken it up upon himself.*"† How great is the happiness contained in these words: "*It is good!*" From the rest of the sentence we may conclude that they embrace everything that is useful, honourable, agreeable, in fact, everything in which happiness may consist. The man that has been accustomed from his youth to the yoke of obedience, will be free throughout life from the crushing yoke of carnal desires. St. Augustine, in the eighth book of his Confessions, acknowledges the difficulty which a soul, that for years had obeyed the concupiscence of the flesh, must experience in shaking off the yoke, and on the other hand he speaks of the facility and the bliss we experience in carrying the yoke of the Lord if the snares of vice have not entrapped the soul. Moreover, it is no inconsiderable gain to obtain merit for every action in the sight of GOD. The man who performs no action of his own free will, but does everything through obedience to his Superior, offers to GOD in each action a sacrifice most pleasing to Him, because as Samuel says: "*Obedience is better than sacrifices.*"‡ St. Gregory gives a reason for this. "In offering victims," he says, "we sacrifice the flesh of another; by obedience our own will is sacrificed."§ And

---
* 1 Kings xv. 22, 23. † Lament. iii. 27, 28. ‡ 1 Kings xv. 23.
§ Lib. *Mor.* xxxv. c. x.

what is still more admirable in this is, that even if a Superior commits a sin in giving any order, a subject not only does not sin, but even obtains merit by his obedience, provided the command itself is not manifestly against the law of GOD. The Prophet goes on to say: "*He shall sit solitary and hold his peace.*" The words mean that the solitary or the obedient man is at rest because he has found peace for his soul. He who has renounced his own will, and has devoted himself entirely to accomplish the Divine will which is manifested to him by the voice of his Superior, desires nothing, seeks for nothing, thinks of nothing, longs for nothing, but is free from all anxious cares, and "*with Mary sits at the Lord's feet hearing His word.*" * The solitary sits down, both because he dwells with those who "*have but one heart and one soul*,"† and because he loves none with a private, individual love, but all in Christ and for the sake of Christ. He is silent because he quarrels with no one, disputes with no one, has litigation with no one. The reason of this great tranquillity is "*because he hath taken it up upon himself,*" and is translated from the ranks of men to the ranks of angels. There are many who busy themselves about themselves, and act like animals devoid of reason. They seek after the things of this world, esteem only those things which delight the senses, feed their carnal desires, and are avaricious, impure, gluttonous, and intemperate. Others lead a purely human life, and remain entirely shut up within themselves, such as those who endeavour to peer into the secrets of nature, or rest satisfied with delivering precepts of morals. Others, again, raise themselves above themselves, and with the special help and assistance of GOD lead a life that is rather angelical than human. These abandon all they possess in this world, and by denying their own wills can say with

* St. Luke x. 39. † Acts iv. 32.

the Apostle: "*Our conversation is in heaven.*"* Emulating the purity, the contemplation, and the obedience of the angels, they lead the life of angels in this world. The angels are never sullied with the stain of sin, "*always see the face of My Father, Who is in heaven,*"† and, disengaged from all things else, are wholly intent on accomplishing the will of GOD. "*Bless the Lord, all ye His angels, you that are mighty in strength, and execute His word, hearkening to the voice of His orders.*"‡ This is the happiness of religious life. Those who on earth imitate as far as possible the purity and obedience of the angels, shall undoubtedly become partakers of their glory in heaven, especially if they follow Christ, their Lord and Master, Who "*humbled Himself, becoming obedient unto death, even the death of the Cross:*" § and "*whereas indeed He was the Son of God, He learned obedience by the things which He suffered:*" ‖ that is, He learned by His own experience that genuine obedience is tried by suffering, and consequently His example not only teaches us obedience, but teaches us that the foundation of true and perfect obedience is humility and patience. It is no proof that we are truly and perfectly obedient in obeying in things that are honourable and pleasant. Such commands do not prove whether it is the virtue of obedience or some other motive that impels us to act. But a man who shows a promptitude and alacrity in obeying in all things that are humiliating and laborious, proves that he is a true disciple of Christ, and has learnt the meaning of true and perfect obedience.

St. Gregory skilfully shows what is necessary to the perfection of obedience in different circumstances. He says: "Sometimes we may receive agreeable, at other times disagreeable commands. It is of the greatest importance to remember that in some circumstances if any-

---

* Philipp. iii. 20. † St. Matt. xviii. 10. ‡ Psalm cii. 20.
§ Philipp. ii. 8. ‖ Heb. v. 8.

thing of self-love creeps into our obedience, our obedience is null; in other circumstances our obedience is less virtuous in proportion as there is less self-sacrifice. For example: a religious is placed in some honourable post, is appointed Superior of a monastery; now if he undertakes this office through the mere human motive of liking it, he will be altogether wanting in obedience. That man is not directed by obedience who in undertaking agreeable duties is the slave of his own ambition. Again, a religious receives some humiliating order, if, for example, when his self-love urges him to aspire to superiority he is ordered to fulfil some office to which neither distinction nor dignity is attached, he will lessen the merit of his obedience in proportion as he fails in forcing his will to desire the post, because unwillingly and by constraint he obeys in a matter which he considers unworthy of his talents or his experience. Obedience invariably loses some of its perfection if the desire for lowly and humble occupation does not in some manner or another accompany the forced obligation of undertaking them. In commands, therefore, which are repugnant to nature, there must be some self-sacrifice, and in commands which are agreeable to nature there must be no self-love. In the former case obedience will be the more meritorious the closer it is united to the Divine will by desires; in the latter case obedience will be the more perfect the more it is separated from any longing for worldly renown. We shall better understand the different marks of true obedience by considering the actions of two saints who are now in heaven.* When Moses was pasturing sheep in the desert, he was called by the Lord, Who spoke to him through the mouth of an angel from the burning bush, to command the Jewish people in their exodus from the land of Egypt. In his humility Moses hesitated about accepting so glorious a command. '*I*

* Exod. iii.

beseech Thee, Lord,' he said, '*I am not eloquent from yesterday and the day before, and since Thou hast spoken to Thy servant I have more impediment and slowness of tongue.*'* He wished to decline the office himself, and begged that it might be given to another. '*I beseech Thee, Lord, send whom Thou wilt send.*' † Behold! he urges his want of eloquence as an excuse to the Author and Giver of speech, to be exonerated from an employment which was honourable and authoritative. St. Paul, as he tells the Galatians,‡ was divinely admonished to go up to Jerusalem. On his journey he meets the Prophet Agabus, and learns from him what he will have to suffer in Jerusalem. '*Agabus, when he was come to us, took Paul's girdle, and binding his own feet and hands he said: Thus saith the Holy Ghost: The man whose girdle this is, the Jews shall bind in this manner in Jerusalem, and shall deliver him into the hands of the Gentiles.*' § Whereupon St. Paul immediately answered, '*I am ready not only to be bound, but to die also in Jerusalem for the name of the Lord Jesus.*' ‖ Undaunted by the revelation he received of the sufferings in store for him, he proceeded to Jerusalem. He really longed to suffer, yet as a man he must have felt some dread; but this very dread was overcome, and rendered him more courageous. Self-love, then, did not find a place in the honourable duty which was imposed upon Moses, because he had to overcome himself in order to assume the command of the Jewish people. Voluntarily did St. Paul set out to meet adversity. He was aware of the persecutions which awaited him, and his fervour made him long for still heavier crosses. The one wished to decline the renown and glory of being the leader of a nation, even when GOD visibly called him; the other was prepared and willing to embrace hardships and tribulations for the love of GOD. With the example

---

* Exod. iv. 10. † Exod. iv. 13. ‡ Gal. ii. 2.
§ Acts xxi. 11. ‖ Acts xxi. 13.

of these two saints before us, we must resolve, if we desire to attain the perfection of obedience, to allow the will of our Superior only to impose honourable employments upon us, and to force our own will to embrace difficult and humiliating offices."* Thus far St. Gregory. Christ our Lord, the Master of all, had previously approved by His conduct the doctrine which St. Gregory here lays down. When He knew the people were coming to take Him away by force and make Him their King, "*He fled into the mountain Himself alone.*" † But when He knew that the Jews and soldiers with Judas at their head were coming to make Him a prisoner and to crucify Him, according to the command which He had received from His Father, He willingly went forth to meet them, and allowed Himself to be captured and bound. Christ therefore, our good Master, has given us an example of the perfection of obedience, not by His preaching and words only, but by His deeds and in truth. He reverenced His Father by an obedience which was founded on suffering and humiliations. The Passion of Christ exhibits the most brilliant example of the most exalted and ennobling of virtues. It is a model which they should ever have before their eyes, who have been called by GOD to aspire to the perfection of obedience and the imitation of Christ.

* Lib. *Mor.* xxxv. c. x. † St. John vi. 15.

Printed in the USA
CPSIA information can be obtained
at www.ICGtesting.com
LVHW081045241123
764823LV00005B/37